Rust and Web3

Master Secure Smart Contracts, DApps, and Consensus Mechanisms

Jeff Cearley

Copyright Page

© 2025 Jeff Cearley

Table of Contents

3

4

Preface

Blockchain technology has transformed how we think about decentralized applications, trustless transactions, and digital ownership. However, building secure and efficient Web3 applications remains a challenge due to the complexity of smart contracts, network protocols, and consensus mechanisms. Developers need a language that prioritizes security, performance, and reliability—this is where **Rust** stands out.

Rust has gained widespread adoption in the Web3 space due to its **memory safety, concurrency model, and efficiency**. It is the language of choice for projects like **Polkadot (Substrate), Solana, and NEAR Protocol**, and is increasingly being used for Ethereum smart contracts via WebAssembly (Wasm).

This book is designed to **bridge the gap between Rust programming and Web3 development**, guiding you through smart contracts, decentralized applications (DApps), and blockchain consensus mechanisms with a focus on best practices and security. Whether you are a **Rust developer looking to enter the Web3 space** or a **blockchain developer wanting to leverage Rust's strengths**, this book provides the knowledge and tools needed to build production-ready applications.

Who This Book Is For

This book is for developers at various levels of experience who want to master **secure blockchain and Web3 development** using Rust. It is particularly suited for:

Rust Developers who want to explore blockchain development, smart contracts, and DApps.

Blockchain Developers who are familiar with Solidity, JavaScript, or Go but want to adopt Rust for better security and performance.

Web3 Enthusiasts who want to understand blockchain consensus mechanisms and how decentralized applications are built.

Software Engineers and Researchers working on next-generation blockchain architectures and scaling solutions.

This book assumes **basic programming knowledge**, but no prior experience with Rust or blockchain is required. Each concept is introduced with **clear explanations, real-world examples, and best practices** to help you apply what you learn.

How This Book Is Structured

This book is structured to provide a **progressive learning experience**, starting with foundational Rust concepts and gradually introducing Web3-specific topics. Each section builds upon the previous one, making it easy to follow regardless of your experience level.

Part 1 covers Rust fundamentals, including ownership, borrowing, async programming, and networking.

Part 2 focuses on writing secure smart contracts using Rust-based frameworks such as Ink! and Solana.

Part 3 explains how to build decentralized applications (DApps) with Rust backends and WebAssembly for frontend integration.

Part 4 explores blockchain consensus mechanisms, custom blockchain development with Substrate, and scaling solutions.

Each chapter contains **clear explanations, code examples, and best practices** to help you apply concepts in real-world development. By the end of this book, you will be able to write secure smart contracts, develop full-stack decentralized applications, and understand how blockchain consensus mechanisms work.

Setting Up Your Development Environment

Before you start building Web3 applications in Rust, it's important to set up the necessary development tools.

1. Install Rust

Rust uses **rustup**, a toolchain manager that simplifies installation and updates. To install Rust, run:

```
curl --proto '=https' --tlsv1.2 -sSf
https://sh.rustup.rs | sh
```
Follow the instructions and restart your terminal. You can verify the installation with:

```
rustc --version
```

2. Install Rust Development Tools

Cargo (Rust's package manager) is installed with Rust.

Rust Analyzer (for better code completion and debugging) can be installed in your editor.

wasm32-unknown-unknown target (for compiling Rust to WebAssembly) can be added with:

```
rustup target add wasm32-unknown-unknown
```

3. Choose an Editor

VS Code (with the Rust extension) is recommended.

JetBrains CLion or IntelliJ IDEA (with the Rust plugin) is a good alternative.

4. Set Up Blockchain-Specific Tools

Depending on the blockchain platform you are targeting, install the necessary tools:

Substrate (for building blockchains):

```
curl https://getsubstrate.io -sSf | bash
```
Solana CLI (for smart contracts on Solana):

```
sh -c "$(curl -sSfL
https://release.solana.com/stable/install)"
```
Ink! CLI (for smart contracts on Polkadot):

```
cargo install cargo-contract
```

5. Test the Installation

To confirm that everything is working, create a simple Rust project:

```
cargo new rust_web3_test
cd rust_web3_test
```

```
cargo run
```
If the program compiles and runs successfully, your Rust development environment is ready.

What You Will Gain from This Book

By working through this book, you will:

✓ Master Rust fundamentals relevant to blockchain development.
✓ Write secure smart contracts using Rust-based frameworks.
✓ Build and deploy decentralized applications (DApps) using Rust and WebAssembly.
✓ Understand blockchain consensus mechanisms and how to implement them.
✓ Gain hands-on experience with real-world blockchain projects.

Web3 is still evolving, and Rust is at the center of this evolution. With the knowledge gained from this book, you will be well-equipped to build **secure, high-performance** blockchain applications that take full advantage of Rust's capabilities.

Let's get started.

Chapter 1: Introduction to Rust and Web3

Blockchain technology is transforming how we interact with the internet. Instead of relying on centralized services owned by a handful of corporations, Web3 introduces a decentralized model where users have direct control over their data, assets, and transactions. But to build secure, efficient, and scalable decentralized applications (DApps), developers need a programming language that prioritizes safety, performance, and reliability.

That's where **Rust** comes in.

In this chapter, we'll break down **what Web3 is, why Rust is the perfect language for blockchain development, and the fundamental concepts you'll encounter in smart contracts, DApps, and consensus mechanisms.**

What is Web3?

The internet has evolved significantly since its creation, shaping how people communicate, share information, and conduct business. Today, the term **Web3** refers to a new phase of internet development that focuses on decentralization, digital ownership, and user control. Unlike earlier versions of the web, which rely on centralized platforms and intermediaries, Web3 is built on blockchain technology, allowing direct peer-to-peer interactions without the need for third parties.

Web3 is often described as the **decentralized web** because it shifts control from corporations to individuals. It enables users to own their data, control their digital identities, and interact with applications in a way that is transparent and resistant to censorship. Smart contracts, which are self-executing agreements written in code, play a key role in this shift by automating transactions and enforcing rules without requiring intermediaries.

To understand Web3, it is helpful to look at how the internet has evolved over time. The earliest phase, now referred to as **Web1**, consisted mainly of static web pages that allowed users to consume information but offered little interaction. Websites were simple, and most users were passive consumers rather than active participants.

This changed with **Web2**, which introduced dynamic and interactive platforms. Social media, online marketplaces, and content-sharing websites made it possible for users to create, share, and engage with digital content. However, these platforms are largely controlled by corporations that collect and monetize user data. While Web2 has enabled significant innovation, it has also raised concerns about privacy, censorship, and centralized control over information and financial transactions.

Web3 addresses these issues by introducing **decentralized networks** powered by blockchain technology. Blockchains function as distributed ledgers, recording transactions in a secure and transparent manner. Unlike traditional databases, which are controlled by a single entity, blockchains are maintained by a network of participants, making them resistant to tampering and censorship. This enables new forms of digital interaction where trust is established through **code and cryptography** rather than through centralized authorities.

One of the defining features of Web3 is **digital ownership**. In traditional online environments, users do not truly own their data or digital assets. For example, content uploaded to a social media platform is ultimately controlled by the company that operates the platform. In contrast, Web3 allows individuals to own their digital assets directly, using technologies such as **non-fungible tokens (NFTs)** and **cryptographic wallets**. These tools enable users to store, transfer, and verify ownership of digital items without relying on intermediaries.

Another key feature of Web3 is the concept of **decentralized applications (DApps)**. Unlike traditional applications that run on centralized servers, DApps operate on blockchain networks, ensuring that they are open, transparent, and resistant to censorship. These applications can facilitate a wide range of activities, including financial services, gaming, identity management, and social networking. Because they are built on open protocols, they encourage collaboration and interoperability, allowing different platforms to interact without proprietary restrictions.

Web3 also introduces new methods of coordination and governance through **decentralized autonomous organizations (DAOs)**. DAOs are community-led entities that make decisions using blockchain-based voting mechanisms. Instead of relying on a central authority, DAOs enable stakeholders to participate in governance, ensuring that decisions are made in a democratic and transparent manner.

One of the most widely discussed aspects of Web3 is **cryptocurrency**. Unlike traditional currencies that are issued and controlled by governments, cryptocurrencies operate on decentralized networks and enable direct peer-to-peer transactions. These digital assets power many Web3 applications, facilitating payments, governance, and incentive mechanisms without the need for banks or financial institutions.

Web3 is still developing, and there are ongoing discussions about its scalability, security, and accessibility. While it presents significant advantages in terms of decentralization and user empowerment, it also introduces challenges, such as regulatory uncertainty and technical complexity. However, its potential to reshape the internet by prioritizing ownership, privacy, and transparency continues to drive innovation in blockchain-based applications.

This new phase of the internet represents a shift in how people interact with technology. By replacing centralized control with decentralized protocols, Web3 enables users to take ownership of their digital presence, participate in decentralized economies, and engage with applications in a more secure and transparent manner. As blockchain technology continues to evolve, Web3 is expected to become a central part of how digital interactions are structured in the future.

The Role of Rust in Blockchain Development

Blockchain technology requires a programming language that prioritizes security, performance, and reliability. Rust has emerged as one of the most effective languages for blockchain development because it offers memory safety, efficient concurrency, and high-speed execution. Many modern blockchain projects, including **Polkadot, Solana, and NEAR Protocol**, have adopted Rust as their primary development language due to these advantages.

Rust provides a strong foundation for building blockchain infrastructure, smart contracts, and decentralized applications (DApps). Unlike older programming languages used in blockchain development, Rust prevents common security vulnerabilities, ensures predictable performance, and allows developers to write scalable and maintainable code.

Why Rust is Ideal for Blockchain Development

Blockchain networks require software that is both **secure** and **efficient**. Since blockchains operate in decentralized environments where software runs across thousands of nodes, any vulnerability can be exploited on a large scale. This makes security a top priority for blockchain developers. Rust helps achieve this through its **strict memory management system, strong type safety, and built-in concurrency model**.

1. Memory Safety Without Garbage Collection

One of Rust's key strengths is its **ownership system**, which manages memory without the need for a garbage collector. In traditional languages like **C and C++**, developers have to manually allocate and free memory, which can lead to **buffer overflows, memory leaks, and segmentation faults**—all of which can introduce security risks.

Rust prevents these issues by enforcing strict rules about how data is accessed and modified. The compiler ensures that:

No data can be accessed after it has been moved or deleted.

Multiple parts of a program cannot modify the same piece of data at the same time unless explicitly allowed.

Memory-related errors are detected at **compile time**, reducing runtime crashes and vulnerabilities.

For blockchain applications, this means fewer bugs, lower security risks, and more **reliable** smart contracts and node software.

2. Concurrency Without Data Races

Concurrency refers to the ability of a program to execute multiple tasks at the same time. Blockchain nodes process thousands of transactions and execute smart contracts **in parallel**. If not handled properly, concurrency can lead to

race conditions, where multiple processes attempt to modify the same data simultaneously, causing unpredictable behavior.

Rust eliminates this issue through **ownership and borrowing rules** that prevent data races at compile time. This ensures that multi-threaded blockchain applications, such as **transaction validators and consensus algorithms**, run efficiently and safely.

3. High Performance and Low Resource Consumption

Rust is a **compiled language**, meaning its code is converted into machine code before execution. This results in **faster performance** compared to interpreted languages like **Python** or **JavaScript**, which require an additional runtime environment.

For blockchain development, high performance is essential because:

Nodes need to **validate transactions quickly** to maintain network efficiency.

Smart contracts must execute with **minimal delay** to avoid excessive transaction fees.

Decentralized applications must handle **high throughput** to support large user bases.

Rust's performance is comparable to **C and C++**, making it an excellent choice for **high-speed blockchain systems**. Unlike Solidity, which runs on the Ethereum Virtual Machine (EVM), Rust can be compiled directly into **WebAssembly (Wasm)**, which is more efficient for blockchain-based execution.

Rust in Smart Contract Development

Smart contracts are **self-executing programs that run on a blockchain**. They automate agreements and enforce rules without requiring a third party. The most widely used language for smart contracts is **Solidity**, which is designed for the Ethereum blockchain. However, Solidity has several security limitations, including **reentrancy attacks, integer overflows, and gas inefficiencies**.

Rust offers a **safer alternative** for smart contract development through **Wasm-based execution environments** like:

13

Ink! – A smart contract framework for **Polkadot and Substrate** networks.

Solana Smart Contracts – Solana uses Rust as its primary language for writing on-chain programs.

NEAR Protocol – Rust is one of the main languages supported for building smart contracts on NEAR.

Using Rust for smart contracts reduces the likelihood of **common vulnerabilities** and improves execution efficiency.

Rust in Blockchain Infrastructure and Consensus Mechanisms

Beyond smart contracts, Rust is widely used for building **blockchain nodes and consensus mechanisms**. A **consensus mechanism** is the algorithm that allows decentralized nodes to agree on the state of the blockchain. Some of the most widely used consensus mechanisms include:

Proof of Work (PoW) – Used by Bitcoin, where miners solve mathematical puzzles to validate transactions.

Proof of Stake (PoS) – Used by Ethereum 2.0, Polkadot, and Solana, where validators are chosen based on the amount of cryptocurrency they hold.

Delegated Proof of Stake (DPoS) – Used by EOS and TRON, where a small group of elected validators confirm transactions on behalf of the network.

Rust is commonly used to **implement these mechanisms** because of its ability to handle **parallel processing**, manage **large amounts of data efficiently**, and prevent **security flaws** in multi-threaded environments.

Projects like **Substrate (the blockchain framework behind Polkadot)** are built entirely in Rust. Substrate allows developers to **create custom blockchains** with modular consensus mechanisms, networking layers, and governance models.

Rust for Decentralized Applications (DApps)

Decentralized applications (DApps) interact with blockchains by sending transactions, retrieving data, and executing smart contracts. While front-end interfaces for DApps are typically written in JavaScript or TypeScript, Rust is often used for:

Backend APIs that handle blockchain interactions efficiently.

WebAssembly (Wasm) modules that allow high-performance smart contracts.

Off-chain computation that processes data without overloading the blockchain.

Rust-based Web3 libraries, such as **ethers-rs** (for Ethereum) and **substrate-api-client** (for Polkadot), allow developers to connect their applications to blockchain networks securely.

Why More Blockchain Projects Are Choosing Rust

Several leading blockchain platforms have adopted Rust for their core development due to its reliability and security. Some of the most well-known projects using Rust include:

Polkadot/Substrate – A blockchain framework that allows developers to create custom blockchains.

Solana – A high-speed blockchain designed for decentralized finance (DeFi) and NFTs.

NEAR Protocol – A scalable blockchain for smart contracts and DApps.

Aleph Zero – A privacy-focused blockchain with fast finality and advanced cryptographic techniques.

The increasing adoption of Rust in blockchain projects highlights its **effectiveness for building secure, high-performance decentralized systems**.

Rust plays a central role in modern blockchain development because it provides **memory safety, high performance, and secure concurrency** without sacrificing efficiency. Its ability to prevent critical security vulnerabilities at compile time makes it an ideal language for building **smart contracts, blockchain nodes, and decentralized applications**.

15

As Web3 continues to evolve, more developers and blockchain platforms are adopting Rust to ensure that decentralized systems remain **secure, scalable, and reliable**. Whether you are building **a new blockchain, optimizing a consensus mechanism, or writing smart contracts**, Rust offers the tools needed to develop high-quality blockchain applications.

Key Features of Rust for Secure Programming

Security is a critical concern in software development, especially in blockchain applications, where vulnerabilities can lead to financial losses and system failures. Rust is designed to help developers write safe, reliable, and efficient code by enforcing strict memory management, preventing data races, and eliminating common security flaws at compile time.

Unlike many programming languages that rely on garbage collection or manual memory management, Rust ensures safety through a **unique ownership system**, strict **type safety**, and **zero-cost abstractions** that prevent common programming errors without sacrificing performance. These features make Rust an excellent choice for blockchain development, where security and efficiency are equally important.

This section explores Rust's core security features and how they contribute to writing safe and maintainable code.

Memory Safety Without Garbage Collection

Memory-related vulnerabilities, such as buffer overflows, use-after-free errors, and null pointer dereferences, are common security risks in traditional languages like C and C++. These issues can lead to unpredictable behavior, system crashes, and security breaches.

Rust prevents these problems using an **ownership system**, which ensures that every value in a program has a single owner at any given time. Ownership rules are enforced at compile time, meaning that memory-related errors are caught before the code runs.

How Ownership Works

16

Ownership in Rust is based on three core principles:

Each value in Rust has a single owner.

When the owner goes out of scope, the value is automatically cleaned up.

Values can be moved or borrowed, but only in ways that ensure safe memory access.

This system eliminates **dangling pointers**, where a reference points to memory that has already been freed, and prevents **double frees**, where the same memory location is freed more than once.

Unlike languages with garbage collection, Rust does not introduce runtime overhead to manage memory. Instead, ownership rules allow memory to be allocated and freed deterministically, improving performance while maintaining safety.

Borrowing and Lifetimes: Preventing Data Races

Concurrency issues, such as **data races**, occur when multiple threads access and modify shared data at the same time without proper synchronization. In many languages, these issues are difficult to detect and debug, often leading to unpredictable behavior and security vulnerabilities.

Rust prevents data races through **borrowing and lifetimes**, which strictly control how references to data are used.

Borrowing Rules

A value can be **borrowed mutably** by one reference at a time.

A value can be **borrowed immutably** by multiple references simultaneously.

A mutable and an immutable reference **cannot coexist** at the same time.

These rules ensure that multiple threads cannot modify the same data simultaneously in an unsafe manner, preventing data corruption and concurrency-related security flaws.

Rust also introduces **lifetimes**, which ensure that references are always valid for as long as they are used. The compiler checks that references do not outlive the data they point to, eliminating **dangling references** and ensuring that memory safety is maintained across function calls and concurrent executions.

Strong Type System and Compile-Time Safety

Rust's type system is designed to catch errors **at compile time,** reducing the risk of runtime failures. This prevents a wide range of bugs that might otherwise go unnoticed in dynamically typed languages like JavaScript or Python.

Key Aspects of Rust's Type Safety

No null values – In Rust, the concept of a null pointer is replaced by the `Option<T>` type, which forces developers to handle the possibility of missing values explicitly. This prevents null pointer dereferences, a common cause of system crashes and security vulnerabilities.

No implicit type conversions – Rust does not allow implicit type conversions between different numeric types, preventing unintended behavior due to silent type mismatches.

Pattern matching and exhaustive checks – Rust enforces exhaustive pattern matching, ensuring that all possible cases in an expression are handled. This reduces the likelihood of unhandled errors.

These features help developers write safer code by making unintended behavior impossible at the language level.

Immutable by Default: Preventing Unintended Modifications

By default, variables in Rust are **immutable,** meaning their values cannot be changed after they are assigned. This prevents unintended modifications and encourages **functional-style programming,** where data transformations occur through explicit operations rather than in-place changes.

Mutability must be explicitly declared using the `mut` keyword. This approach forces developers to think carefully about when and how data is modified, reducing the likelihood of accidental changes that could lead to security flaws.

In blockchain applications, immutability is crucial for ensuring that **smart contracts execute consistently** and that **blockchain state remains secure.**

Rust's default immutability provides an additional layer of protection against unintended state modifications.

Error Handling with `Result` and `Option`

Rust enforces **safe error handling** through its `Result<T, E>` and `Option<T>` types, which require developers to handle failures explicitly. This prevents silent failures and reduces the risk of unhandled exceptions that could compromise security.

`Result<T, E>`: Handling Operations That May Fail

Rust does not use exceptions for error handling. Instead, functions that may fail return a `Result<T, E>` type, where:

`T` is the expected successful result.

`E` is the error type if the operation fails.

Developers must explicitly handle both success and failure cases, preventing issues where errors are ignored or crash the program unexpectedly.

`Option<T>`: Handling Missing Values Safely

Instead of using null values, Rust provides `Option<T>`, which represents either:

`Some(T)`, indicating a valid value.

`None`, indicating the absence of a value.

Because `Option<T>` forces developers to handle the case where a value may not exist, it eliminates null pointer errors and makes code safer.

In blockchain applications, error handling is particularly important for **transaction validation**, **smart contract execution**, and **network communication**. Rust's explicit error management ensures that failures are handled gracefully rather than leading to security vulnerabilities.

Safe Concurrency with `Send` and `Sync` Traits

Concurrency in Rust is **safe by design** due to its strict borrowing rules, but it also provides additional safeguards through its **`Send` and `Sync` traits**. These traits define how data can be shared between threads, preventing unsafe access patterns that could lead to data corruption.

`Send` **ensures that data can be safely transferred between threads.** If a type does not implement `Send`, it cannot be moved across threads, preventing unintended sharing of non-thread-safe data.

`Sync` **ensures that multiple threads can safely reference the same data.** If a type does not implement `Sync`, it cannot be accessed concurrently without proper synchronization mechanisms.

These rules ensure that Rust programs are free from **race conditions and deadlocks**, making it an excellent choice for multi-threaded blockchain systems that require high security and reliability.

Why These Features Matter for Blockchain Development

Blockchain applications must handle **complex financial transactions, cryptographic operations, and decentralized consensus mechanisms**. Any security vulnerability in these systems can result in **loss of funds, system failures, or network attacks**. Rust's safety features provide several advantages for blockchain development:

Eliminates memory-related vulnerabilities that have historically led to blockchain hacks.

Prevents concurrency issues that could affect transaction validation and network security.

Ensures predictable performance without runtime overhead, making it suitable for high-performance blockchain nodes.

Encourages secure smart contract development, reducing the risk of logic errors and vulnerabilities.

Many blockchain projects, including **Polkadot, Solana, and NEAR**, use Rust for these reasons. Its safety guarantees and performance optimizations make it an ideal choice for developers building secure, high-quality blockchain applications.

Rust provides a strong foundation for secure programming through **ownership-based memory management, strict type safety, safe concurrency, and explicit error handling**. These features ensure that Rust applications are **less prone to security vulnerabilities, more efficient, and easier to maintain**.

For blockchain developers, Rust's design helps create **robust smart contracts, secure transaction processing systems, and high-performance blockchain nodes**. As blockchain technology continues to evolve, Rust remains a preferred choice for developers seeking security and reliability in decentralized applications.

Overview of Smart Contracts, DApps, and Consensus

Blockchain technology enables decentralized applications that operate without a central authority. Three fundamental concepts that make this possible are **smart contracts, decentralized applications (DApps), and consensus mechanisms**.

Smart contracts allow agreements to be executed automatically when predefined conditions are met.

DApps use smart contracts to provide decentralized services, similar to traditional applications but without reliance on centralized servers.

Consensus mechanisms ensure that transactions are verified and recorded in a secure and trustless manner.

Understanding these concepts is essential for building reliable and efficient blockchain-based applications. This section explains how they function and why they are critical to the development of decentralized systems.

Smart Contracts

A **smart contract** is a self-executing program stored on a blockchain. It automatically enforces rules and executes actions based on predefined conditions, without requiring intermediaries.

Smart contracts replace traditional agreements in many areas, including finance, supply chain management, and digital identity verification. Because they run on decentralized networks, they are resistant to **tampering, fraud, and censorship**.

How Smart Contracts Work

A smart contract follows a simple **if-then structure**. When a specific condition is met, the contract executes the corresponding action.

For example, in a **decentralized lending application**, a smart contract might be programmed as follows:

If a borrower deposits collateral, then they receive a loan.

If the borrower fails to repay the loan by the deadline, then the collateral is transferred to the lender.

Since the rules are written in code and stored on the blockchain, **neither party can alter or dispute the terms once the contract is deployed**.

Key Features of Smart Contracts

Decentralization – Unlike traditional contracts that rely on a trusted authority (such as a bank or a lawyer), smart contracts execute on a decentralized blockchain network.

Security – Once deployed, smart contracts cannot be changed, reducing the risk of fraud. However, security flaws in the contract's code can be exploited, which is why secure programming practices are essential.

Transparency – The contract's code and execution are visible to all participants, ensuring fairness.

Efficiency – Automated execution eliminates the need for manual processing, reducing costs and delays.

Languages Used for Smart Contracts

Different blockchain platforms support different programming languages for writing smart contracts.

Ethereum uses **Solidity**, which is optimized for execution on the Ethereum Virtual Machine (EVM).

Polkadot and Substrate-based blockchains use **Ink!**, which is written in **Rust** and compiled to WebAssembly (Wasm).

Solana supports **Rust-based smart contracts**, which are compiled directly into machine code for efficiency.

NEAR Protocol also supports Rust for writing smart contracts using the Wasm runtime.

By leveraging Rust-based smart contracts, developers can create more secure and efficient applications compared to traditional Solidity-based systems.

Decentralized Applications (DApps

A **decentralized application (DApp)** is a software application that interacts with a blockchain network through smart contracts. Unlike traditional applications that rely on centralized servers, DApps run on distributed blockchain networks, making them more resistant to **censorship, downtime, and unauthorized control**.

Characteristics of a DApp

A DApp differs from traditional applications in several ways:

Decentralization – Data and application logic are stored on a blockchain rather than on a single server.

Smart Contracts – The backend logic is executed by smart contracts, which automate interactions between users.

Open Source – Many DApps are open source, allowing anyone to verify and contribute to the code.

Token-Based Economy – Many DApps use blockchain-based tokens for governance, transactions, or rewards.

DApp Architecture

A typical DApp consists of three layers:

Smart Contract Layer – Contains the core logic of the application, written in a blockchain-compatible programming language.

Backend Layer – Handles off-chain computations, data processing, and external APIs. This layer is often written in **Rust, Go, or Python**.

Frontend Layer – Provides the user interface, usually built with **JavaScript, TypeScript, or React** and connected to the blockchain through Web3 libraries.

Examples of DApps

DApps exist in various industries, offering decentralized alternatives to traditional services:

Decentralized Finance (DeFi): Platforms like **Uniswap** and **Aave** allow users to trade, lend, and borrow cryptocurrencies without banks.

Gaming and NFTs: Games like **Axie Infinity** use blockchain to enable true ownership of in-game assets.

Decentralized Social Networks: Applications like **Lens Protocol** provide censorship-resistant social media platforms.

Supply Chain Management: Blockchain-based tracking systems ensure transparency in global supply chains.

Rust plays a crucial role in DApp development by providing **secure, high-performance backends** and enabling efficient smart contract execution on blockchains that support WebAssembly (Wasm).

Consensus Mechanisms

A **consensus mechanism** is the process by which nodes in a blockchain network agree on the validity of transactions. Since blockchains operate without a central authority, they require a system to ensure that all participants maintain a single, agreed-upon version of the blockchain.

Different consensus mechanisms determine how transactions are validated and how new blocks are added to the blockchain.

Common Consensus Mechanisms

Proof of Work (PoW)

PoW is the consensus mechanism used by **Bitcoin**. In PoW, miners compete to solve complex mathematical puzzles, and the first to find a solution earns the right to add a new block to the blockchain.

Pros: High security and resistance to attacks.

Cons: High energy consumption and slower transaction processing.

Proof of Stake (PoS)

PoS is an alternative consensus mechanism where validators are chosen based on the number of tokens they hold and are willing to "stake" as collateral. **Ethereum 2.0, Polkadot, and Solana** use PoS variations to validate transactions.

Pros: More energy-efficient and faster than PoW.

Cons: Wealthier participants have more influence over the network.

Delegated Proof of Stake (DPoS)

In DPoS, token holders vote for a small group of validators to secure the network. This system is used by blockchains like **EOS and TRON**.

Pros: High transaction speed and efficiency.

Cons: Centralization risks due to a limited number of validators.

Byzantine Fault Tolerance (BFT) Variants

Some blockchains use **BFT-based consensus mechanisms,** such as **Tendermint (Cosmos)** and **HotStuff (Libra/Diem)**, which allow nodes to reach agreement even if some behave maliciously.

Pros: High-speed finality and low energy consumption.

Cons: Requires a predefined number of validators.

Consensus and Rust-Based Blockchains

Rust is commonly used in consensus algorithm development because of its **thread safety, efficiency, and memory management capabilities**. Examples include:

25

Polkadot (Substrate Framework): Uses Rust to build custom consensus mechanisms.

Solana: Uses Rust to support its high-performance Proof of History (PoH) consensus model.

Cosmos SDK: Implements consensus mechanisms in Rust for some blockchain modules.

Consensus mechanisms ensure that blockchain networks remain **secure, decentralized, and efficient**. Choosing the right consensus model depends on the specific goals of the blockchain, such as scalability, security, or decentralization.

Smart contracts, decentralized applications, and consensus mechanisms are the foundation of blockchain technology. Smart contracts automate transactions without intermediaries, DApps provide decentralized services, and consensus mechanisms maintain security and trust in blockchain networks.

Rust plays an important role in **securing and optimizing** these components by providing **safe memory management, efficient concurrency handling, and high performance**. As blockchain technology continues to grow, Rust will remain a key tool for developers building secure and scalable decentralized systems.

Chapter 2: Rust Fundamentals for Blockchain Development

Blockchain development requires a programming language that is both **secure and efficient**. Rust stands out because it enforces **memory safety, prevents data races, and optimizes performance** without relying on garbage collection. These features are essential when writing blockchain applications, where even a small mistake can lead to **security vulnerabilities, performance bottlenecks, or unintended behavior** in smart contracts and decentralized applications (DApps).

Before building blockchain systems with Rust, it's important to understand **core Rust concepts** that make it unique:

Understanding Ownership and Borrowing in Rust

Rust introduces a unique approach to memory management that ensures safety and efficiency without relying on a garbage collector. This approach is centered around **ownership and borrowing**, two fundamental concepts that define how data is accessed and managed within a Rust program.

If you're coming from other programming languages like C++, Python, or Java, you might be used to managing memory manually or relying on a garbage collector to handle deallocation. Rust takes a different approach, enforcing memory safety **at compile time** through strict rules. These rules prevent issues like **null pointer dereferences, use-after-free errors, and data races**, which are common sources of security vulnerabilities and program crashes.

Understanding **ownership and borrowing** is essential for writing efficient Rust programs, especially in blockchain development, where performance and security are equally important. In this section, we will **explore ownership and borrowing in depth, examine how Rust enforces these rules, and work through practical examples that demonstrate their importance**.

Ownership: The Foundation of Rust's Memory Safety

Ownership in Rust is a **set of rules that govern how memory is allocated and freed**. It ensures that every value in a program has a single owner at any given time. When that owner goes out of scope, Rust automatically deallocates the value, preventing memory leaks and dangling pointers.

Rust enforces three key ownership rules:

Each value in Rust has a single owner.

When the owner goes out of scope, the value is dropped.

A value can only be moved from one owner to another.

To see ownership in action, consider the following example:

```
fn main() {
    let transaction = String::from("Block #1: Alice
sent 10 BTC to Bob"); // transaction owns the
string
    let record = transaction; // ownership is moved
to record

    // println!("{}", transaction); // X ERROR:
transaction is no longer valid
    println!("{}", record); // ✅ Works: record now
owns the value
}
```

In this example, `transaction` initially owns the string `"Block #1: Alice sent 10 BTC to Bob"`. When we assign `transaction` to `record`, **ownership is transferred**, and `transaction` is no longer valid. If we attempt to access `transaction` after ownership has moved, Rust will **throw a compile-time error** to prevent undefined behavior.

This rule prevents issues like **use-after-free**, where a variable is accessed after it has been deallocated. Unlike languages where invalid memory access might result in unpredictable behavior, Rust ensures that these errors are caught **before the program even runs**.

Transferring Ownership in Function Calls

Ownership is also transferred when passing values to functions:

```
fn process_transaction(tx: String) {
    println!("Processing transaction: {}", tx);
} // tx is dropped here

fn main() {
    let tx = String::from("Alice paid 5 ETH to
Charlie");
    process_transaction(tx); // Ownership moves
into the function

    // println!("{}", tx); // ✗ ERROR: tx is no
longer valid
}
```

Once ownership is moved into the function `process_transaction`, `tx` is no longer accessible in `main()`. Rust ensures that the value is **dropped** once the function execution completes, preventing memory leaks.

This might seem restrictive at first, but it forces developers to **think explicitly about ownership**, reducing bugs that arise from unintended data sharing.

Borrowing: Allowing Multiple Accesses Without Moving Ownership

If ownership always moved when passing values around, it would be difficult to write reusable functions. **Borrowing** solves this by allowing multiple functions to access a value **without transferring ownership**.

Immutable Borrowing: Read-Only Access

Borrowing allows references to be passed into functions instead of moving the actual value. A **reference** is indicated by &, and it enables a function to access a value **without taking ownership**.

```
fn view_transaction(tx: &String) {
    println!("Viewing transaction: {}", tx);
}

fn main() {
    let tx = String::from("Charlie sent 2 BTC to
Dave");

    view_transaction(&tx); // Borrowing the value
```

```
    println!("Transaction still exists: {}", tx);
// ✅ Works because ownership was not moved
}
```

In this case, `tx` is **borrowed** by the `view_transaction` function. Because it is an **immutable reference**, the function can **read** the value but **cannot modify it**.

Mutable Borrowing: Modifiable Access

Rust also allows **mutable borrowing**, where a function is permitted to **modify** the borrowed value. However, there is a strict rule:

→ **Only one mutable reference can exist at a time** to prevent race conditions and unexpected modifications.

```
fn update_transaction(tx: &mut String) {
    tx.push_str(" - Confirmed");
}

fn main() {
    let mut tx = String::from("Dave received 3 ETH
from Eve");

    update_transaction(&mut tx); // Mutable borrow
    println!("Updated transaction: {}", tx);
}
```

Here, `tx` is **borrowed mutably** by the function, which allows it to append - `Confirmed` to the transaction record.

However, Rust prevents multiple mutable references at the same time:

```
fn main() {
    let mut tx = String::from("Block #5");

    let ref1 = &mut tx;
    let ref2 = &mut tx; // ✗ ERROR: Cannot borrow
mutably more than once

    println!("{}", ref1);
}
```

This rule **eliminates data races** and ensures that data is not modified simultaneously from different parts of the program.

Why Ownership and Borrowing Matter in Blockchain Development

Blockchain applications must handle **large amounts of transaction data, cryptographic signatures, and network communication efficiently**. Memory safety is critical because any vulnerability could lead to **security breaches, data corruption, or loss of digital assets**.

1. Preventing Data Corruption in Blockchain Nodes

Blockchain nodes process transactions **in parallel**, validating multiple inputs from different sources. If two processes try to modify the same blockchain state at the same time, it can lead to inconsistent data. Rust prevents these errors through **safe borrowing rules**, ensuring that only one part of the program modifies data at a time.

2. Secure Smart Contracts Execution

Smart contracts handle **financial transactions and critical business logic**. If a contract has a memory-related vulnerability, attackers can exploit it to **drain funds or manipulate data**. Rust's ownership model eliminates **buffer overflows, dangling pointers, and race conditions**, making smart contracts **more secure**.

3. Efficient Data Structures for Blockchain Storage

Rust ensures that blockchain data structures, such as **Merkle trees, cryptographic hashes, and transaction ledgers**, are managed efficiently. Borrowing allows developers to pass references to these data structures without duplicating large amounts of memory, improving performance.

Exercises: Test Your Understanding

To reinforce these concepts, try solving the following exercises:

1. Fix the Ownership Error
The following program has an ownership issue. Modify it to compile correctly.

```
fn process(tx: String) {
    println!("Processing: {}", tx);
```

```
}

fn main() {
    let transaction = String::from("Alice paid 10
BTC to Bob");
    process(transaction);
    println!("Still available: {}", transaction);
// ✗ ERROR
}
```

2. Convert to Borrowing

Modify the previous exercise so that the `process` function borrows the transaction instead of taking ownership.

Ownership and borrowing are **core principles in Rust** that ensure memory safety without requiring a garbage collector. Ownership **prevents memory leaks and dangling pointers**, while borrowing **allows multiple functions to access data without unnecessary copying**.

For blockchain developers, these concepts are essential because they provide **secure, efficient, and high-performance memory management**. Mastering **ownership and borrowing** will allow you to build **faster, safer blockchain systems** that can process transactions reliably at scale.

Memory Safety and Performance in Rust

When writing software, two of the most critical factors are **memory safety** and **performance**. In blockchain applications, where efficiency and security are paramount, failing to manage memory properly can lead to serious vulnerabilities, inefficiencies, and even catastrophic failures.

Many traditional programming languages force developers to choose between **manual memory management (which can lead to errors like buffer overflows and memory leaks)** or **automatic garbage collection (which can introduce performance overhead and unpredictable delays)**. Rust takes a different approach.

Rust enforces **memory safety at compile time** through a strict ownership and borrowing system. It allows developers to write highly efficient code without worrying about memory corruption, unsafe access, or performance bottlenecks. Rust achieves this without requiring a garbage collector, making it ideal for high-performance applications like **blockchain nodes, cryptographic operations, and smart contract execution**.

Why Memory Safety Matters

Memory safety refers to a program's ability to **prevent memory access errors** such as:

Null pointer dereferences (accessing memory that isn't allocated).

Use-after-free errors (accessing memory that has already been deallocated).

Buffer overflows (writing data past the allocated memory boundary).

Race conditions (multiple threads accessing memory in an unpredictable manner).

In many programming languages, **these errors lead to security vulnerabilities, crashes, or unpredictable behavior**. In blockchain applications, where data integrity is essential, even a small memory bug can **corrupt transaction data, cause smart contract failures, or open security loopholes for attackers**.

For example, in **C or C++**, developers must manually allocate and free memory. If they forget to free memory after using it, the program **leaks memory over time**. If they free it too early, the program may **crash when trying to access freed memory**. These issues can be extremely difficult to debug and fix.

How Rust Ensures Memory Safety

Rust prevents memory errors **before they happen** by enforcing strict rules **at compile time**. These rules ensure that:

Memory is **automatically cleaned up** when it is no longer needed.

Variables can only be accessed in a **safe and predictable manner**.

There are **no dangling references** or illegal memory accesses.

Rust does this through its **ownership system**, which ensures that every value in the program has a single owner at any given time. When the owner goes out of scope, Rust automatically deallocates the memory.

Example: Preventing Use-After-Free Errors

In **C++**, a common mistake is freeing memory too early, leading to **use-after-free errors**.

```
#include <iostream>

void freeMemory(int* ptr) {
    delete ptr;  // Manually deallocating memory
}

int main() {
    int* num = new int(42);
    freeMemory(num);
    std::cout << *num;  // ✗ ERROR: Accessing
memory after it was freed
}
```

This can lead to unpredictable behavior, crashes, or even security vulnerabilities.

Rust **prevents this mistake entirely** because ownership rules ensure that a value **cannot be accessed after being moved or dropped**.

```
fn main() {
    let num = Box::new(42); // Box allocates memory
on the heap
    drop(num); // Memory is explicitly freed

    // println!("{}", num); // ✗ ERROR: num was
moved and cannot be used
}
```

By enforcing memory safety **at compile time**, Rust eliminates an entire class of security risks without requiring a garbage collector.

No Null Pointers: Eliminating a Common Source of Bugs

Many languages allow **null pointers**, which can lead to **null reference errors** when a program tries to access an object that doesn't exist.

For example, in **Java**, the following code compiles but crashes at runtime:

```
String message = null;
System.out.println(message.length()); // ✗ ERROR:
Null pointer dereference
```

Rust eliminates this issue by **not allowing null values at all**. Instead, Rust provides the `Option<T>` type, which forces developers to handle missing values explicitly.

```
fn get_message() -> Option<String> {
    None // Represents a missing value
}

fn main() {
    let message = get_message();

    match message {
        Some(text) => println!("Message: {}",
text),
        None => println!("No message found."), //
    Explicitly handling the missing value
    }
}
```

This ensures that programs handle null-like conditions **safely and predictably**, reducing crashes and unexpected behavior.

Rust's Performance: Faster Execution Without Garbage Collection

Many modern programming languages use **garbage collection (GC)** to automatically reclaim unused memory. While this simplifies development, **it comes at a cost**:

Garbage collectors pause program execution at unpredictable times, causing performance spikes.

Memory usage is often higher because the program doesn't immediately free memory when it's no longer needed.

Fine-grained memory control is difficult, making it harder to optimize performance-sensitive applications.

Rust **avoids garbage collection entirely**. Instead, it manages memory **deterministically** through ownership rules, allowing the program to free memory exactly when it is no longer needed. This results in:

☑ **Lower latency**, since there are no unexpected GC pauses.

☑ **More efficient memory usage**, because memory is freed immediately when ownership ends.

☑ **Better control over performance**, which is crucial for high-throughput applications like blockchain nodes.

Example: Rust vs. Garbage-Collected Languages

Let's consider an application that processes thousands of blockchain transactions per second.

A language with garbage collection (e.g., Java or Go) may suddenly pause execution when the garbage collector runs, causing delays in transaction validation.

Rust processes each transaction and frees memory immediately, ensuring smooth and predictable performance.

For blockchain systems that require **low-latency and high-speed processing**, Rust's **predictable memory management** makes a huge difference.

Using Rust's Smart Pointers for Efficient Memory Management

Rust provides **smart pointers** that allow fine-grained control over memory while maintaining safety guarantees.

Box: Storing Data on the Heap

A `Box<T>` allows a value to be stored on the heap instead of the stack. This is useful when working with **large data structures** that should not be copied.

```
fn main() {
```

```
    let blockchain_data = Box::new("Block #10: 50
BTC transferred");
    println!("{}", blockchain_data);
} // ✓ blockchain_data is automatically freed when
it goes out of scope
```

Rc: Shared Ownership

The Rc<T> type allows multiple parts of a program to share ownership of the same data. This is useful when multiple parts of a blockchain system need access to shared data.

```
use std::rc::Rc;

fn main() {
    let transaction = Rc::new("Transaction ID:
12345".to_string());

    let user1 = Rc::clone(&transaction);
    let user2 = Rc::clone(&transaction);

    println!("{}", user1); // ✓ Both user1 and
user2 share ownership
    println!("{}", user2);
}
```

Because Rc<T> keeps track of how many references exist, Rust knows exactly when it is safe to free the memory.

Exercises: Test Your Understanding

1. Prevent the Ownership Error

The following Rust program has an ownership issue. Modify it to compile correctly.

```
fn use_memory(data: String) {
    println!("{}", data);
}

fn main() {
    let info = String::from("Blockchain
Transaction");
```

```
    use_memory(info);
    println!("{}", info); // ✗ ERROR: Ownership
moved
}
```

2. Convert to Borrowing

Modify the function above to borrow the value instead of taking ownership.

Rust's approach to **memory safety and performance** makes it one of the best languages for blockchain development. It eliminates **memory errors, prevents security vulnerabilities, and ensures predictable execution speeds**—all without requiring a garbage collector.

By understanding **ownership, borrowing, and Rust's efficient memory management**, developers can build **faster, more secure blockchain systems** that process transactions reliably at scale.

Data Structures: Structs, Enums, and Pattern Matching

Programming requires organizing and managing data in a structured and efficient way. In blockchain applications, where transactions, blocks, and accounts contain multiple fields of related data, structuring this information correctly is essential. Rust provides powerful tools to handle structured data through **structs, enums, and pattern matching**.

If you've worked with other languages, you might already be familiar with similar concepts. Structs in Rust function like **objects or records** in other languages, allowing you to group related data. Enums let you **define multiple possible variants of a type**, ensuring clear and explicit handling of different cases. Pattern matching enables **powerful and expressive ways** to work with both structs and enums, helping you write **concise, safe, and readable** code.

These concepts form the backbone of many Rust applications, and understanding them deeply is important for blockchain development. Whether you're representing a **block, a smart contract function, or a transaction**

38

type, choosing the right data structure helps ensure your program is **efficient, maintainable, and free from logical errors**.

Structs: Grouping Related Data Together

A **struct** in Rust allows you to group multiple pieces of related information into a single logical unit. This is useful in blockchain applications where a transaction, a block, or an account consists of several attributes that belong together.

Defining and Using Structs

Let's consider a basic transaction in a blockchain system. A transaction typically contains details such as **who is sending funds, who is receiving them, and the amount being transferred**.

In Rust, this information can be represented using a struct:

```rust
struct Transaction {
    sender: String,
    receiver: String,
    amount: u64,
}

fn main() {
    let tx = Transaction {
        sender: String::from("Alice"),
        receiver: String::from("Bob"),
        amount: 100,
    };

    println!("Transaction: {} sent {} coins to {}",
tx.sender, tx.amount, tx.receiver);
}
```

Here's what happens in the code above:

A struct called `Transaction` **is defined**, grouping related attributes together.

A transaction instance (tx) is created, with specific values assigned to `sender`, `receiver`, and `amount`.

The transaction data is printed, showing how information can be accessed using `tx.sender`, `tx.receiver`, and `tx.amount`.

By using a struct, all the details about a transaction are **bundled into a single object**, making the code **more organized and readable**.

Struct Methods: Adding Behavior to Structs

Structs in Rust can also have **methods** associated with them. This is useful when you want to perform operations related to the data inside the struct.

For example, let's say we want a method that **verifies whether a transaction amount is valid** (greater than zero).

```rust
struct Transaction {
    sender: String,
    receiver: String,
    amount: u64,
}

impl Transaction {
    fn is_valid(&self) -> bool {
        self.amount > 0
    }
}

fn main() {
    let tx = Transaction {
        sender: String::from("Alice"),
        receiver: String::from("Bob"),
        amount: 50,
    };

    println!("Is transaction valid? {}",
tx.is_valid());
}
```

Here's what this code does:

We define a method is_valid inside an `impl` block.

The method checks if the transaction amount is greater than zero and returns a boolean value.

Calling tx.is_valid() lets us check if a transaction is valid before processing it.

Methods on structs make it easy to bundle **both data and related behavior** together, improving **code organization and clarity**.

Enums: Defining Multiple Variants of a Type

An **enum** in Rust allows you to define a **type that can have multiple possible values**, known as **variants**. This is useful when working with blockchain data where an item can have **different types or states**.

For example, a blockchain may have different types of transactions, such as:

A standard transfer of funds from one account to another.

A minting transaction that creates new coins.

A burn transaction that permanently removes coins from circulation.

Instead of handling this with separate structs, an enum provides a clean and structured way to represent all possible types of transactions.

Defining and Using Enums

```rust
enum TransactionType {
    Transfer { sender: String, receiver: String,
amount: u64 },
    Mint { recipient: String, amount: u64 },
    Burn { sender: String, amount: u64 },
}

fn main() {
    let tx1 = TransactionType::Transfer {
        sender: String::from("Alice"),
        receiver: String::from("Bob"),
        amount: 100,
    };

    let tx2 = TransactionType::Mint {
        recipient: String::from("Charlie"),
        amount: 50,
    };

    let tx3 = TransactionType::Burn {
        sender: String::from("Dave"),
        amount: 20,
```

41

```
    };
}
```

Each transaction type has a **distinct structure**, and Rust enforces **strict type safety**, preventing accidental misuse.

Pattern Matching: Handling Structs and Enums Effectively

Pattern matching allows you to **process different variants of an enum in a safe and structured way.** This is particularly useful when handling different transaction types in a blockchain.

Using `match` to Handle Enums

```
fn process_transaction(tx: TransactionType) {
    match tx {
        TransactionType::Transfer { sender,
receiver, amount } => {
            println!("Transfer: {} sent {} coins to
{}", sender, amount, receiver);
        }
        TransactionType::Mint { recipient, amount }
=> {
            println!("Minted {} coins for {}",
amount, recipient);
        }
        TransactionType::Burn { sender, amount } =>
{
            println!("Burn: {} destroyed {} coins",
sender, amount);
        }
    }
}

fn main() {
    let tx = TransactionType::Transfer {
        sender: String::from("Alice"),
        receiver: String::from("Bob"),
        amount: 100,
    };

    process_transaction(tx);
}
```

Here's what happens:

42

The `match` statement evaluates the transaction type and executes the corresponding block of code.

Each variant is handled explicitly, preventing unintentional behavior.

Rust enforces that all possible variants must be covered, ensuring robustness.

This approach makes **handling different transaction types safe and predictable**, reducing errors when processing blockchain transactions.

Why Structs, Enums, and Pattern Matching Matter in Blockchain Development

Blockchain applications handle **large amounts of structured data**, including transactions, blocks, and smart contracts. Using **structs and enums correctly** ensures that this data is organized efficiently and safely.

Structs keep related data together, making blockchain records easy to manage.

Enums allow precise handling of different types of blockchain operations, reducing ambiguity.

Pattern matching ensures clear and safe processing, making sure that every case is accounted for.

By applying these concepts correctly, developers can write **secure, efficient, and maintainable blockchain systems**.

Exercises: Test Your Understanding

Create a Struct for a Blockchain Block
Define a `Block` struct that contains a **block number, a list of transactions, and a hash**. Implement a method that prints block details.

Modify the `TransactionType` Enum
Add a new transaction type: **ContractCall**, which includes a `contract_address` and a `function_name`. Update the `match` function to handle this new case.

Rust's **structs, enums, and pattern matching** provide powerful tools for organizing and processing blockchain data. Structs help **group related fields**, enums allow **handling multiple transaction types**, and pattern matching ensures **safe and structured processing**.

Mastering these tools will help you build **secure, high-performance blockchain applications** that handle transactions and smart contracts efficiently.

Traits and Generics in Blockchain Programming

Blockchain applications need to be **modular, flexible, and reusable**. Whether you're developing a blockchain framework, a smart contract system, or a cryptographic protocol, your code should handle different **data types** and **behaviors** without unnecessary duplication.

Rust provides two powerful features that help achieve this: **traits and generics**.

Traits allow you to define shared behavior across different types. Instead of writing separate implementations for every type that needs a particular functionality, you define a trait once and implement it for multiple types.

Generics let you write code that works with different data types **without sacrificing type safety or performance**.

These features are especially useful in blockchain programming, where many components—transactions, consensus algorithms, smart contracts—must follow specific rules while remaining flexible enough to accommodate different implementations.

Traits: Defining Shared Behavior in Blockchain Systems

A **trait** in Rust is similar to an **interface in Java** or an **abstract class in C++**. It defines a set of methods that **must be implemented by any type that adopts the trait**.

In blockchain programming, traits help **standardize functionality across different types**. For example, a blockchain might have different types of transactions, but all transactions must be able to **verify themselves** before being included in a block.

Defining a Trait

Let's define a trait called `Validatable`, which enforces that any type implementing it must have a `validate` method.

```
trait Validatable {

    fn validate(&self) -> bool;

}
```

This trait does **not** provide an implementation. Instead, it defines a **contract** that any implementing type must follow.

Implementing a Trait for a Transaction Struct

A blockchain transaction should have a way to **validate itself**—for example, by checking that the amount is greater than zero. We can enforce this requirement by implementing the `Validatable` trait for a `Transaction` struct.

```
struct Transaction {
    sender: String,
    receiver: String,
    amount: u64,
}

impl Validatable for Transaction {
    fn validate(&self) -> bool {
        self.amount > 0
    }
}

fn main() {
    let tx = Transaction {
        sender: String::from("Alice"),
        receiver: String::from("Bob"),
        amount: 100,
    };
```

```
        println!("Is transaction valid? {}",
tx.validate());
}
```

Here's how it works:

The **Validatable trait is defined** with a single method, `validate`.

The **Transaction struct is created**, holding details about a blockchain transaction.

The **Validatable trait is implemented for Transaction**, ensuring that every transaction can check if it is valid.

The validate method checks if the transaction amount is greater than zero.

If you try to create a `Transaction` and call `validate()`, Rust ensures that the function is **always available**, because the struct **must** implement the `Validatable` trait.

Using Traits for Blockchain Components

Traits are particularly useful in **blockchain consensus algorithms**. Different blockchains use different consensus mechanisms (like **Proof of Work, Proof of Stake, or Byzantine Fault Tolerance**), but they all follow some common principles:

A consensus mechanism must be able to **validate transactions**.

It must be able to **propose and verify new blocks**.

Instead of writing separate logic for each consensus type, we can define a **trait** that sets a common interface.

```
trait Consensus {
    fn validate_block(&self, block_hash: &str) ->
bool;
    fn propose_block(&self) -> String;
}

struct ProofOfWork;

impl Consensus for ProofOfWork {
```

```rust
    fn validate_block(&self, block_hash: &str) ->
bool {
        block_hash.starts_with("000") // Example
condition for a valid block
    }

    fn propose_block(&self) -> String {
        String::from("New block with Proof of
Work")
    }
}

fn main() {
    let pow = ProofOfWork;

    println!("Is block valid? {}",
pow.validate_block("000123abc"));
    println!("Proposal: {}", pow.propose_block());
}
```

This approach makes it easy to **extend** the system with additional consensus mechanisms (such as Proof of Stake) without modifying the existing logic.

Generics: Writing Flexible and Reusable Blockchain Code

A **generic** in Rust allows a function or struct to work with **multiple data types** without sacrificing type safety. This is especially useful in blockchain applications, where data structures may need to handle **different types of cryptographic signatures, transactions, or consensus rules**.

Generics **reduce code duplication** by letting a single function or struct **work with multiple types**, while still enforcing strong type safety at compile time.

Using Generics in a Blockchain Block Structure

Let's define a **generic block** that can hold any type of transaction.

```rust
struct Block<T> {
    transactions: Vec<T>,
    hash: String,
}
```

47

```
impl<T> Block<T> {
    fn new(transactions: Vec<T>, hash: String) ->
Self {
        Block { transactions, hash }
    }
}

fn main() {
    let txs = vec![
        String::from("Alice -> Bob: 50 BTC"),
        String::from("Charlie -> Dave: 20 BTC"),
    ];

    let block = Block::new(txs,
String::from("000abc123"));

    println!("Block Hash: {}", block.hash);
}
```

This implementation makes the `Block` struct **generic**, meaning it can store **any type of transaction**. If later we introduce a new transaction type, we don't need to modify the `Block` struct—**it works with all types automatically**.

Combining Traits and Generics for Maximum Flexibility

Generics and traits **work well together** to create highly flexible blockchain components. A common pattern is using **traits with generics** to enforce behavior while allowing type flexibility.

For example, let's create a **generic blockchain** that enforces a validation rule on all transactions, regardless of type.

```
trait Validatable {
    fn validate(&self) -> bool;
}

struct Blockchain<T: Validatable> {
    transactions: Vec<T>,
}

impl<T: Validatable> Blockchain<T> {
    fn new(transactions: Vec<T>) -> Self {
        Blockchain { transactions }
```

```rust
    }

    fn validate_all(&self) -> bool {
        self.transactions.iter().all(|tx|
tx.validate())
    }
}

struct Transaction {
    sender: String,
    receiver: String,
    amount: u64,
}

impl Validatable for Transaction {
    fn validate(&self) -> bool {
        self.amount > 0
    }
}

fn main() {
    let tx1 = Transaction {
        sender: String::from("Alice"),
        receiver: String::from("Bob"),
        amount: 50,
    };

    let tx2 = Transaction {
        sender: String::from("Charlie"),
        receiver: String::from("Dave"),
        amount: 30,
    };

    let blockchain = Blockchain::new(vec![tx1,
tx2]);

    println!("Are all transactions valid? {}",
blockchain.validate_all());
}
```

In this implementation:

A Blockchain struct is defined with a generic type T.

The generic type T is constrained to types that implement `Validatable`, ensuring that only validatable transactions can be added.

The `validate_all` **method ensures every transaction in the blockchain is valid.**

This design ensures that **only valid transactions** can be processed, while keeping the blockchain **flexible enough to support different types of transactions**.

Traits and generics are powerful tools for writing **scalable, flexible, and reusable blockchain applications**. Traits define **shared behavior**, ensuring that different blockchain components follow the same rules, while generics allow code to **adapt to multiple types** without duplication.

By mastering these concepts, developers can create **secure, efficient blockchain systems** that can evolve as technology advances.

Chapter 3: Asynchronous Programming in Rust

Blockchain networks are inherently **distributed and concurrent**. Thousands of nodes process transactions, validate blocks, and communicate with each other in real-time. To build efficient blockchain applications, developers must handle **multiple tasks simultaneously**—network requests, transaction validation, consensus mechanisms, and smart contract execution—all while maintaining speed and security.

This is where **asynchronous programming** comes in.

Rust provides **async programming** features that allow applications to perform multiple operations **without blocking execution**. Unlike traditional multi-threading, which creates separate threads for concurrent tasks, async programming in Rust **uses a single thread efficiently** to perform many operations at once.

Concurrency in Blockchain Systems

Blockchain networks operate on a global scale, where thousands of independent nodes communicate, validate transactions, and reach consensus on new blocks. Unlike traditional applications that process tasks sequentially, blockchain software must handle multiple operations at the same time. This includes **processing incoming transactions, validating cryptographic proofs, maintaining network communication, and executing smart contracts**—all without compromising performance or security.

Handling these tasks efficiently requires a solid understanding of **concurrency**. In simple terms, concurrency allows multiple operations to execute at the same time, improving system responsiveness and throughput. Rust provides **safe and efficient concurrency features** that help blockchain applications process data in parallel while avoiding memory issues, deadlocks, and race conditions.

In this section, we will explore **why concurrency is essential for blockchain systems, how Rust's concurrency model works, and how to write** concurrent blockchain applications using Rust's async features and multi-threading capabilities.

Why Concurrency Matters in Blockchain Development

A blockchain system processes a **continuous flow of transactions and blocks**. Without concurrency, every operation would have to wait for the previous one to complete before starting. This would severely limit the number of transactions that can be processed per second, making the system slow and inefficient.

Consider a scenario where a blockchain node needs to:

Accept transactions from multiple users and add them to a mempool (a waiting area for unconfirmed transactions).

Validate transactions in parallel to ensure they follow protocol rules.

Broadcast transactions to other nodes in the network.

Process and verify incoming blocks while continuing to accept new transactions.

If all of these tasks were executed **sequentially**, the network would quickly become overwhelmed, causing delays and bottlenecks. By using concurrency, a blockchain node can **perform all of these tasks simultaneously**, ensuring that the system remains responsive and scalable.

Concurrency in Blockchain Nodes

Each blockchain node is responsible for several core functions that require concurrency:

Transaction Processing

When users submit transactions to the network, they must be **validated and stored in the mempool** until they are included in a block. A concurrent system ensures that multiple transactions can be processed at the same time, rather than forcing each one to wait for the previous transaction to complete.

Consensus Mechanism Execution

Blockchain networks use different **consensus algorithms** (such as Proof of Work, Proof of Stake, or Byzantine Fault Tolerance) to agree on the state of the ledger. These mechanisms require nodes to exchange messages, verify cryptographic proofs, and propose new blocks—all of which happen concurrently.

For example, in **Proof of Stake (PoS)**, multiple validators participate in leader selection and block proposal at the same time. A well-designed system will run these processes concurrently to maximize efficiency.

Networking and Peer-to-Peer Communication

Blockchain nodes constantly send and receive data from other nodes. They must relay transactions, sync block data, and listen for network messages—all while continuing to validate transactions and execute smart contracts. Without concurrency, a node would pause processing every time it communicates with another node, significantly slowing down the system.

Rust's Concurrency Model

Rust provides several powerful tools for writing **safe and efficient concurrent programs**. Unlike many other programming languages, Rust prevents **race conditions, deadlocks, and undefined behavior** at **compile time**, ensuring that multi-threaded blockchain applications are both reliable and performant.

Ownership and Borrowing in Concurrent Code

Traditional multi-threading often leads to **data races**, which occur when multiple threads try to modify the same data at the same time. Rust eliminates this issue by enforcing **ownership and borrowing rules** that prevent unsafe memory access.

Rust ensures that:

A variable can either have **one mutable reference** or **multiple immutable references**, but not both at the same time.

Data shared between threads must be **explicitly marked as thread-safe** using types like `Arc<T>` and `Mutex<T>`.

53

This approach **prevents race conditions before the code even compiles**, making Rust an ideal choice for building concurrent blockchain systems.

Using Async in Rust for Blockchain Concurrency

Rust's `async` and `await` syntax provides a structured way to write concurrent code **without creating multiple threads**. This is useful for blockchain applications that need to handle thousands of simultaneous operations **efficiently, without blocking execution**.

Example: Processing Transactions Concurrently

A blockchain node must process many transactions at once. Using Rust's async model, we can write a function that handles transactions **asynchronously**:

```
use tokio::time::{sleep, Duration};

async fn process_transaction(tx: &str) {
    println!("Processing transaction: {}", tx);
    sleep(Duration::from_secs(2)).await; //
Simulating processing time
    println!("Transaction completed: {}", tx);
}

#[tokio::main]
async fn main() {
    let transactions = vec![
        "Alice -> Bob: 10 BTC",
        "Charlie -> Dave: 5 BTC",
        "Eve -> Frank: 2 BTC",
    ];

    let futures: Vec<_> =
transactions.iter().map(|&tx|
process_transaction(tx)).collect();
    futures::future::join_all(futures).await; //
Process all transactions concurrently
}
```

In this example:

Each transaction is processed asynchronously, without waiting for others to complete.

The `sleep` function simulates **real transaction processing delays**, such as cryptographic validation.

`join_all(futures).await` ensures that all transactions complete **in parallel**.

This approach enables blockchain nodes to **process thousands of transactions per second**, improving network scalability.

Multi-Threading for High-Performance Blockchain Applications

While async programming is great for **I/O-bound tasks** (such as network communication and transaction handling), some blockchain operations are **CPU-intensive** and require actual multi-threading. This includes:

Cryptographic operations (e.g., hashing, signing, key generation).

Mining (Proof of Work) where multiple threads must compute hashes in parallel.

Parallel block validation in high-performance blockchain implementations.

Rust's `std::thread` module provides **safe and efficient multi-threading**.

Example: Mining a Block Using Multiple Threads

```
use std::thread;
use std::sync::{Arc, Mutex};

fn mine_block(block_data: &str) -> String {
    format!("{} - mined", block_data) // Simulating
Proof of Work
}

fn main() {
    let block_data =
Arc::new(Mutex::new(vec!["Block 1", "Block 2",
"Block 3"]));
    let mut handles = vec![];
```

```
    for _ in 0..3 {
        let data = Arc::clone(&block_data);
        let handle = thread::spawn(move || {
            let mut blocks = data.lock().unwrap();
            if let Some(block) = blocks.pop() {
                let mined_block =
mine_block(block);
                println!("{}", mined_block);
            }
        });
        handles.push(handle);
    }

    for handle in handles {
        handle.join().unwrap();
    }
}
```

This example:

Uses multiple **threads to mine blocks in parallel**.

Prevents data corruption using **Arc (Atomic Reference Counting) and Mutex (Mutual Exclusion)**.

Ensures that **each block is processed safely without race conditions**.

This technique is useful for **optimizing blockchain performance** while ensuring memory safety.

Challenges of Concurrency in Blockchain

While concurrency improves performance, **it also introduces complexity**. Developers must carefully design blockchain applications to **avoid issues such as**:

Data races: Rust prevents these at compile time, but incorrect use of `Mutex<T>` or `Arc<T>` can still cause deadlocks.

Synchronization overhead: Too much locking can slow down execution. Smart use of async tasks and thread pools can minimize contention.

Network bottlenecks: Even with concurrent processing, **network latency can be a limiting factor**. Using efficient transport protocols and caching techniques can help mitigate this.

Properly balancing **concurrent execution and synchronization** is key to building a **secure, scalable blockchain system**.

Concurrency is at the core of modern blockchain systems. Rust's **async programming and multi-threading capabilities** provide the tools needed to **handle high transaction throughput, validate blocks efficiently, and communicate with peers in real-time**. By leveraging Rust's safe concurrency model, blockchain developers can create **secure, high-performance decentralized applications** that scale effectively.

Using async and await in Rust

Asynchronous programming allows a program to handle multiple tasks at the same time without blocking execution. In blockchain development, where a node must process incoming transactions, validate blocks, and communicate with peers simultaneously, async programming is essential for maintaining efficiency and scalability.

Rust's **async and await** syntax makes writing concurrent code easier by allowing functions to run **asynchronously**, meaning they don't stop execution while waiting for a task to complete. This prevents bottlenecks and ensures that the system remains responsive even under heavy load.

Many programming languages support asynchronous execution, but Rust's **ownership model and memory safety features** make its async implementation unique. It eliminates issues such as **race conditions, memory leaks, and deadlocks**, which are common pitfalls in concurrent systems. In this section, we will explore how async and await work in Rust, how they improve performance in blockchain applications, and how to use them effectively.

In traditional synchronous programming, each operation must complete before the next one starts. If a blockchain node is fetching data from a peer, it must

57

wait for the response before doing anything else. This delay can slow down transaction processing and network communication.

With async programming, tasks can be started **without waiting** for them to finish. Instead of pausing execution, Rust's async functions return a **future**, which represents a computation that will complete later. The program can continue executing other tasks in the meantime.

Blocking Execution in a Synchronous Function

In this example, a function processes a transaction but **blocks** execution for two seconds while doing so.

```
use std::thread;
use std::time::Duration;

fn process_transaction(tx: &str) {
    println!("Processing transaction: {}", tx);
    thread::sleep(Duration::from_secs(2)); //
Simulates a delay
    println!("Transaction completed: {}", tx);
}

fn main() {
    println!("Starting transactions...");
    process_transaction("Alice -> Bob: 10 BTC");
    process_transaction("Charlie -> Dave: 5 BTC");
    println!("All transactions processed.");
}
```

Each transaction is processed **one at a time**, meaning the second transaction must wait for the first one to complete. This approach is inefficient when dealing with a high volume of transactions.

Non-Blocking Execution Using Async and Await

Now, let's rewrite the function using async and await to allow **concurrent execution**.

```
use tokio::time::{sleep, Duration};

async fn process_transaction(tx: &str) {
    println!("Processing transaction: {}", tx);
```

```
    sleep(Duration::from_secs(2)).await; //
Simulates a delay
    println!("Transaction completed: {}", tx);
}

#[tokio::main]
async fn main() {
    println!("Starting transactions...");

    let tx1 = process_transaction("Alice -> Bob: 10
BTC");
    let tx2 = process_transaction("Charlie -> Dave:
5 BTC");

    tokio::join!(tx1, tx2); // Runs both
transactions concurrently

    println!("All transactions processed.");
}
```

Here's what happens:

The **async function** `process_transaction` runs **without blocking execution**.

The `await` keyword tells Rust **to pause this function** until the delay is complete, but other tasks can continue running.

The `tokio::join!` macro **executes both transactions concurrently**, reducing wait time.

With this approach, multiple transactions are processed at the same time, improving throughput and responsiveness.

How Async and Await Work in Rust

To understand **async and await**, it's important to break down how Rust handles asynchronous execution.

Async Functions and Futures

In Rust, an `async fn` does not execute immediately. Instead, it returns a **future**—a placeholder for a value that will become available later. The future does nothing until it is explicitly awaited.

59

```
async fn example() -> String {
    "Async function executed".to_string()
}

#[tokio::main]
async fn main() {
    let result = example().await; // Wait for the
function to complete
    println!("{}", result);
}
```

By using `.await`, we tell Rust to **wait** for the future to complete before moving on. However, if a function is **not awaited**, it won't execute.

Running Multiple Async Tasks Efficiently

If you need to run multiple async tasks, using `.await` one after another still **executes them sequentially**, which isn't always efficient. To execute them **concurrently**, you can use **Tokio's join! macro**.

```
async fn task1() {
    println!("Task 1 started...");
    sleep(Duration::from_secs(3)).await;
    println!("Task 1 completed.");
}

async fn task2() {
    println!("Task 2 started...");
    sleep(Duration::from_secs(2)).await;
    println!("Task 2 completed.");
}

#[tokio::main]
async fn main() {
    tokio::join!(task1(), task2());
    println!("Both tasks finished.");
}
```

In this example, **both tasks run at the same time**. Task 2 finishes first, but Task 1 continues running until it is complete.

This method is useful for blockchain nodes that need to **validate transactions while fetching new blocks from the network**.

Using Async for Blockchain Networking

Blockchain nodes must communicate with peers, relay transactions, and synchronize data. Rust's async system is ideal for **handling multiple network connections simultaneously**.

Creating an Async TCP Server

A blockchain node often listens for incoming connections from peers. The following example sets up an **async TCP server** using Tokio:

```
use tokio::net::TcpListener;
use tokio::io::{AsyncReadExt, AsyncWriteExt};

#[tokio::main]
async fn main() {
    let listener =
TcpListener::bind("127.0.0.1:8080").await.unwrap();
    println!("Blockchain node listening on port
8080...");

    loop {
        let (mut socket, _) =
listener.accept().await.unwrap();
        tokio::spawn(async move {
            let mut buffer = [0; 1024];
            let bytes_read = socket.read(&mut
buffer).await.unwrap();
            println!("Received: {}",
String::from_utf8_lossy(&buffer[..bytes_read]));

            socket.write_all(b"Transaction
received").await.unwrap();
        });
    }
}
```

Here's how it works:

The node **listens for incoming connections** using `TcpListener::bind()`.

When a peer connects, `listener.accept().await` **waits without blocking** other operations.

The connection is handled in a separate async task using `tokio::spawn`, allowing **multiple peers to connect simultaneously**.

This ensures that a blockchain node can **process network requests concurrently**, rather than blocking the entire system for each connection.

Common Mistakes When Using Async in Rust

When working with async code, it's important to avoid common mistakes that can lead to performance issues.

Not Using .await

An async function won't run unless it is explicitly awaited. The following code does **nothing** because `fetch_data()` is never awaited:

```
async fn fetch_data() -> String {
    "Blockchain data received".to_string()
}

fn main() {
    fetch_data(); // ✗ Does nothing
}
```
The correct way to call it:
```
#[tokio::main]
async fn main() {
    let data = fetch_data().await; // ✓ Now it runs
    println!("{}", data);
}
```

Blocking the Async Runtime

Using `std::thread::sleep()` inside an async function **blocks execution** and prevents other async tasks from running. Instead, always use `tokio::time::sleep()`.

```
async fn delay() {

tokio::time::sleep(Duration::from_secs(2)).await;
// ✓ Non-blocking
}
```

Async programming in Rust is essential for **building high-performance blockchain applications**. By using **async functions and await**, developers can create systems that **handle multiple transactions, process network requests, and synchronize blockchain data without blocking execution**.

Rust's async model ensures that blockchain applications remain **scalable, responsive, and efficient**, allowing nodes to **process thousands of transactions per second** while maintaining stability.

Networking with Tokio and async-std

Blockchain networks are built on **peer-to-peer (P2P) communication**, where nodes exchange transactions, broadcast blocks, and maintain synchronization with the network. Unlike traditional client-server architectures, blockchain nodes must handle **multiple simultaneous connections**, often needing to send and receive data asynchronously without blocking execution.

In Rust, **Tokio** and **async-std** provide robust tools for writing efficient, non-blocking network applications. These libraries allow developers to handle multiple network connections concurrently, making them perfect for building blockchain nodes, decentralized applications, and high-performance transaction processing systems.

Networking in Rust follows an **asynchronous model**, meaning functions **do not block execution** while waiting for data. Instead, they return a **future**, which represents an operation that will complete later. This allows Rust applications to **handle thousands of network requests concurrently without creating unnecessary threads**.

Why Asynchronous Networking?

A blockchain node must:

Accept incoming connections from other peers.

Send and receive transactions without blocking other operations.

Synchronize the blockchain state by downloading and verifying new blocks.

Respond to API requests from wallets or smart contract platforms.

If a node used **synchronous networking**, it would be forced to **wait** for each request to complete before handling the next one. This would slow down transaction processing and limit scalability.

With **asynchronous networking**, multiple connections are handled **simultaneously**, allowing a node to remain responsive even under heavy load.

Building an Async TCP Server with Tokio

A blockchain node needs to **listen for incoming connections** from other peers. The following example demonstrates how to create an **asynchronous TCP server** using Tokio.

Setting Up Tokio

To use Tokio in a Rust project, add the following dependencies to `Cargo.toml`:

```
[dependencies]
tokio = { version = "1", features = ["full"] }
```

Tokio provides an **async runtime** that allows multiple tasks to run concurrently without blocking execution.

Implementing the TCP Server

```
use tokio::net::TcpListener;
use tokio::io::{AsyncReadExt, AsyncWriteExt};

#[tokio::main]
async fn main() {
    let listener =
TcpListener::bind("127.0.0.1:8080").await.unwrap();
    println!("Blockchain node listening on port
8080...");

    loop {
        let (mut socket, _) =
listener.accept().await.unwrap();
        tokio::spawn(async move {
            let mut buffer = [0; 1024];
            let bytes_read = socket.read(&mut
buffer).await.unwrap();
```

```
                println!("Received: {}",
String::from_utf8_lossy(&buffer[..bytes_read]));

            socket.write_all(b"Transaction
received").await.unwrap();
        });
    }
}
```

How This Works

The **TCP server binds to** `127.0.0.1:8080`, listening for incoming connections.

When a new connection is established, `listener.accept().await` **waits asynchronously** for a client to connect.

The connection is handled in a **new async task using** `tokio::spawn`, ensuring that **multiple peers can connect simultaneously**.

The node **reads data from the client** and **sends a response** asynchronously.

This setup enables a blockchain node to handle **multiple transactions and block propagation events in parallel**, improving network efficiency.

Building an Async TCP Client with Tokio

A blockchain node also needs to **connect to other nodes** to fetch transaction data and synchronize blocks. The following example shows how to create an **asynchronous TCP client** that connects to a server and sends transaction data.

```
use tokio::net::TcpStream;
use tokio::io::{AsyncWriteExt, AsyncReadExt};

#[tokio::main]
async fn main() {
    let mut stream =
TcpStream::connect("127.0.0.1:8080").await.unwrap()
;
    stream.write_all(b"New transaction: Alice ->
Bob: 10 BTC").await.unwrap();

    let mut buffer = [0; 1024];
```

65

```
    let bytes_read = stream.read(&mut
buffer).await.unwrap();
    println!("Server response: {}",
String::from_utf8_lossy(&buffer[..bytes_read]));
}
```

How This Works

The client **connects to the server** using `TcpStream::connect()`.

It **sends transaction data asynchronously** using `write_all().await`.

It **reads the server's response asynchronously**, allowing it to process multiple messages **without blocking execution**.

By using asynchronous networking, a blockchain node can **send and receive data concurrently**, keeping it responsive even under high transaction volume.

Building an Async TCP Server with async-std

Tokio is **not the only** async library in Rust. **async-std** provides a similar API, designed to feel like Rust's standard library but with async support.

To use async-std, add this to `Cargo.toml`:

```
[dependencies]
async-std = { version = "1", features =
["attributes"] }
```

Implementing a TCP Server with async-std

```
use async_std::net::TcpListener;
use async_std::prelude::*;
use async_std::task;

#[async_std::main]
async fn main() -> std::io::Result<()> {
    let listener =
TcpListener::bind("127.0.0.1:8081").await?;
    println!("Blockchain node listening on port
8081...");

    while let Some(stream) =
listener.incoming().next().await {
```

```
        let mut stream = stream?;
        task::spawn(async move {
            let mut buffer = vec![0u8; 1024];
            let bytes_read = stream.read(&mut
buffer).await.unwrap();
            println!("Received: {}",
String::from_utf8_lossy(&buffer[..bytes_read]));

            stream.write_all(b"Transaction
acknowledged").await.unwrap();
        });
    }
    Ok(())
}
```

This example works **similarly to the Tokio version**, but uses async-std's async runtime.

Choosing Between Tokio and async-std

Both Tokio and async-std are excellent for asynchronous networking, but they have different strengths.

Tokio is the **most widely used async framework** in Rust and is optimized for **high-performance, low-latency applications** like blockchain nodes. It is used in **major Rust projects**, including the **Rust async ecosystem and Web3 frameworks**.

async-std is **simpler and more lightweight**, making it ideal for smaller async applications or projects that require a **standard-library-like experience**.

For blockchain applications that require **scalability, fast networking, and complex concurrency management, Tokio is the preferred choice**.

Handling WebSockets in Blockchain Networking

Blockchain applications also require **WebSockets** for real-time communication, such as live transaction streaming or event notifications. Rust provides excellent support for WebSockets through libraries like tokio-tungstenite.

Here's a simple WebSocket server using **Tokio and tungstenite**:

67

```rust
use
tokio_tungstenite::tungstenite::protocol::Message;
use tokio::net::TcpListener;
use tokio_tungstenite::accept_async;
use futures_util::{StreamExt, SinkExt};

#[tokio::main]
async fn main() {
    let listener =
TcpListener::bind("127.0.0.1:9001").await.unwrap();
    println!("WebSocket server running on
ws://127.0.0.1:9001");

    while let Ok((stream, _)) =
listener.accept().await {
        tokio::spawn(async move {
            let ws_stream =
accept_async(stream).await.unwrap();
            let (mut write, mut read) =
ws_stream.split();

            while let Some(Ok(msg)) =
read.next().await {
                println!("Received: {:?}", msg);

write.send(Message::Text("Acknowledged".into())).aw
ait.unwrap();
            }
        });
    }
}
```

This WebSocket server allows blockchain applications to **broadcast live events** without requiring constant polling from clients.

Networking is at the core of **blockchain infrastructure**, enabling **transactions, block propagation, and peer-to-peer communication**. By using **async networking with Tokio and async-std**, blockchain applications can handle **thousands of concurrent connections efficiently**, ensuring scalability and responsiveness.

Rust's **safe and efficient async runtime** makes it one of the best languages for building **high-performance decentralized networks**.

68

Handling Transactions and Events in Blockchain Systems

In any blockchain network, transactions are at the core of its functionality. Users send transactions to transfer assets, execute smart contracts, or interact with decentralized applications. The network must efficiently handle incoming transactions, validate them, and ensure they are securely recorded on the blockchain.

At the same time, blockchain systems rely on an **event-driven model**, where nodes listen for updates—such as new transactions, mined blocks, or smart contract state changes—and respond accordingly. Events allow decentralized applications to react to blockchain changes in real-time, ensuring that wallets, exchanges, and other services stay synchronized with the network. Rust provides powerful tools for handling transactions and events **asynchronously**, ensuring that blockchain nodes remain efficient, scalable, and responsive even under heavy transaction loads.

A transaction in a blockchain typically contains the following key elements:

Sender – The address of the account initiating the transaction.

Receiver – The address of the recipient.

Amount – The quantity of assets being transferred.

Signature – A cryptographic proof verifying that the sender authorized the transaction.

Nonce – A unique identifier to prevent double-spending.

Timestamp – The time when the transaction was created.

Before a transaction is added to a block, it must go through several stages:

Transaction Creation – A user or smart contract generates a transaction and signs it with a private key.

Transaction Submission – The signed transaction is broadcasted to the network.

69

Mempool Storage – Each node temporarily stores unconfirmed transactions in a mempool.

Validation – Nodes check that the transaction is correctly signed, has sufficient balance, and is not a duplicate.

Transaction Propagation – Valid transactions are shared with other nodes in the network.

Block Inclusion – A miner or validator selects transactions from the mempool, groups them into a block, and proposes the block to the network.

Each step must be **handled efficiently and concurrently** to maintain high throughput, prevent congestion, and ensure security.

Building a Transaction Processing System in Rust

Rust's **async programming model** allows blockchain nodes to process multiple transactions simultaneously **without blocking execution**. Let's implement an asynchronous transaction processing system using Rust.

Defining the Transaction Struct

To start, we define a **struct** to represent a blockchain transaction:

```
use serde::{Serialize, Deserialize};

#[derive(Debug, Serialize, Deserialize, Clone)]
struct Transaction {
    sender: String,
    receiver: String,
    amount: u64,
    signature: String,
    timestamp: u64,
}
```

Each transaction contains information about the sender, receiver, amount, and a cryptographic signature to verify authenticity.

Asynchronously Processing Incoming Transactions

Blockchain nodes must **listen for new transactions and validate them** before adding them to the mempool. To handle this concurrently, we use **Tokio's async runtime**.

```rust
use tokio::sync::mpsc;
use tokio::time::{sleep, Duration};

async fn validate_transaction(tx: Transaction) ->
bool {
    println!("Validating transaction from {} to {}
for {} coins...", tx.sender, tx.receiver,
tx.amount);
    sleep(Duration::from_secs(1)).await; //
Simulate computational work
    true // Assume all transactions are valid for
this example
}

async fn process_transaction_queue(mut receiver:
mpsc::Receiver<Transaction>) {
    while let Some(tx) = receiver.recv().await {
        if validate_transaction(tx.clone()).await {
            println!("Transaction from {} processed
successfully!", tx.sender);
        } else {
            println!("Transaction from {} failed
validation.", tx.sender);
        }
    }
}

#[tokio::main]
async fn main() {
    let (tx_sender, tx_receiver) =
mpsc::channel(10); // Queue for pending
transactions


tokio::spawn(process_transaction_queue(tx_receiver)
);

    let sample_tx = Transaction {
        sender: "Alice".to_string(),
        receiver: "Bob".to_string(),
        amount: 100,
        signature: "sample_signature".to_string(),
```

71

```
        timestamp: 1676543200,
    };

    tx_sender.send(sample_tx).await.unwrap();
}
```

Here's what this system does:

Transactions are added to a queue using a message-passing channel (`mpsc::channel`).

An async task (`process_transaction_queue`) continuously listens for new transactions and processes them as they arrive.

Each transaction is validated asynchronously using the `validate_transaction` function.

With this design, a blockchain node can **handle multiple transactions in parallel** without blocking execution, improving efficiency and scalability.

Handling Events in Blockchain Systems

Events in a blockchain system are **notifications triggered by specific actions**, such as:

A new block being mined.

A transaction being confirmed.

A smart contract executing a function.

Applications listen for these events to **stay updated** with blockchain activity. For example, a **crypto exchange** might listen for transactions involving its users, while a **wallet application** updates the user's balance whenever a new transaction is confirmed.

Rust's **Tokio and async channels** allow us to implement event-driven systems that **broadcast blockchain events asynchronously**.

Implementing an Event Notification System

Let's create an event system where a node **notifies listeners** when a new transaction is added to the mempool.

```
use tokio::sync::broadcast;
```

```rust
use tokio::time::{sleep, Duration};

#[derive(Debug, Clone)]
struct BlockchainEvent {
    event_type: String,
    details: String,
}

async fn event_listener(mut receiver:
broadcast::Receiver<BlockchainEvent>) {
    while let Ok(event) = receiver.recv().await {
        println!("Received event: {} - {}",
event.event_type, event.details);
    }
}

#[tokio::main]
async fn main() {
    let (tx, _) = broadcast::channel(10); //
Broadcast channel for events

    let listener1 = tx.subscribe();
    let listener2 = tx.subscribe();

    tokio::spawn(event_listener(listener1));
    tokio::spawn(event_listener(listener2));

    sleep(Duration::from_secs(2)).await;

    let new_event = BlockchainEvent {
        event_type:
"TransactionReceived".to_string(),
        details: "Alice -> Bob: 50
BTC".to_string(),
    };

    tx.send(new_event.clone()).unwrap();
}
```

This system:

Uses **Tokio's broadcast channel** to notify multiple listeners of blockchain events.

73

Allows **multiple subscribers** to listen for the same event.

Ensures that each listener **receives the latest blockchain updates asynchronously**.

This approach is useful for **building real-time dashboards, monitoring tools, and Web3 applications** that need to react to blockchain activity in real-time.

Putting It All Together: End-to-End Transaction Handling and Event Emission

Let's combine transaction processing with event handling so that every time a transaction is validated, an event is broadcasted to notify other parts of the system.

```rust
use tokio::sync::{mpsc, broadcast};
use tokio::time::{sleep, Duration};

#[derive(Debug, Clone)]
struct Transaction {
    sender: String,
    receiver: String,
    amount: u64,
}

#[derive(Debug, Clone)]
struct BlockchainEvent {
    event_type: String,
    details: String,
}

async fn validate_transaction(tx: Transaction,
event_sender: broadcast::Sender<BlockchainEvent>) {
    println!("Validating transaction from {} to
{}...", tx.sender, tx.receiver);
    sleep(Duration::from_secs(1)).await;

    let event = BlockchainEvent {
        event_type:
"TransactionValidated".to_string(),
```

```rust
        details: format!("Transaction from {} to {}
confirmed", tx.sender, tx.receiver),
    };

    event_sender.send(event).unwrap();
}

async fn transaction_handler(mut receiver:
mpsc::Receiver<Transaction>, event_sender:
broadcast::Sender<BlockchainEvent>) {
    while let Some(tx) = receiver.recv().await {
        validate_transaction(tx,
event_sender.clone()).await;
    }
}

#[tokio::main]
async fn main() {
    let (tx_sender, tx_receiver) =
mpsc::channel(10);
    let (event_sender, mut event_receiver) =
broadcast::channel(10);

    tokio::spawn(transaction_handler(tx_receiver,
event_sender.clone()));

    let sample_tx = Transaction {
        sender: "Alice".to_string(),
        receiver: "Bob".to_string(),
        amount: 100,
    };

    tx_sender.send(sample_tx).await.unwrap();

    while let Ok(event) =
event_receiver.recv().await {
        println!("Received blockchain event: {:?}",
event);
    }
}
```

With this, a blockchain node can **validate transactions, process them asynchronously, and notify listeners** in real-time, making the system **highly efficient and event-driven**.

Chapter 4: Smart Contract Development with Rust

Smart contracts are **self-executing programs** that run on a blockchain, enabling **automated, trustless transactions** without intermediaries. They power **decentralized applications (DApps), financial protocols, supply chain systems, and governance mechanisms**, making them one of the most impactful innovations in blockchain technology.

Rust has emerged as a **leading language** for smart contract development due to its **memory safety, performance, and strong type system**. While Solidity is widely used for Ethereum, Rust is the primary language for **next-generation blockchain platforms** such as **Polkadot (Ink!), Solana, and NEAR Protocol**.

Introduction to Smart Contracts

A **smart contract** is a self-executing program stored on a blockchain that runs when predefined conditions are met. It automates agreements between parties without requiring intermediaries such as banks, lawyers, or centralized authorities. This automation ensures that transactions are secure, transparent, and irreversible.

Smart contracts play a crucial role in **decentralized finance (DeFi), supply chain management, identity verification, non-fungible tokens (NFTs), and many other blockchain applications**. They enable trustless interactions, meaning that participants do not need to rely on a central entity to enforce rules—**the blockchain does that automatically**.

How Smart Contracts Work

A smart contract follows a simple **"if-then" logic**. It contains a set of predefined rules coded by a developer. When a user submits a transaction that meets these conditions, the contract executes its programmed response.

For example, consider a **decentralized escrow service** using a smart contract:

If Buyer sends payment, then **Seller receives funds**.

If the product is not delivered within a specified time, then **Buyer gets a refund**.

Once deployed, a smart contract is **immutable**, meaning its logic cannot be altered. This guarantees that transactions are **executed exactly as programmed**, eliminating fraud and disputes.

Key Properties of Smart Contracts

1. Decentralization

Smart contracts run on **distributed blockchain networks**, meaning no single entity has control over execution. Instead of relying on a central server, multiple nodes (computers in the network) validate and execute the contract, ensuring transparency and security.

2. Automation

A smart contract **automatically executes** when conditions are met, removing the need for manual processing. This reduces the risk of human error and minimizes administrative costs.

3. Transparency

All smart contract transactions are recorded on a **public ledger**, allowing anyone to audit and verify the contract's behavior. This level of transparency increases trust between parties.

4. Security

Because smart contracts operate on a **blockchain**, they benefit from cryptographic security. Once deployed, a smart contract cannot be modified, protecting it from tampering and unauthorized access. However, vulnerabilities in the contract's code can be exploited, making **secure coding practices essential**.

5. Trustless Execution

Smart contracts **remove the need for trust between parties**. The contract's logic is enforced by the blockchain network, so parties do not have to rely on each other to follow through on agreements.

Common Use Cases for Smart Contracts

Smart contracts are widely used across various industries, transforming traditional processes by making them more **efficient, cost-effective, and secure**.

1. Decentralized Finance (DeFi)

DeFi platforms use smart contracts to provide **financial services without banks or intermediaries**. These include:

Lending and borrowing – Users can lend crypto assets and earn interest or borrow funds with collateral.

Automated trading – Decentralized exchanges (DEXs) allow peer-to-peer asset trading.

Yield farming – Users can earn rewards by providing liquidity to DeFi platforms.

2. Supply Chain Management

Smart contracts improve **supply chain transparency** by tracking products from manufacturer to consumer.

Automated payments – A manufacturer can receive payment when a shipment is verified.

Tamper-proof tracking – Each step of the supply chain is recorded on the blockchain, ensuring authenticity.

3. Non-Fungible Tokens (NFTs)

NFTs use smart contracts to verify **ownership and authenticity of digital assets**, such as artwork, music, and virtual goods.

Proof of ownership – Ensures that digital assets cannot be duplicated or forged.

Automated royalties – Artists receive a percentage of sales every time their NFT is resold.

4. Voting Systems

Smart contracts enable **secure, tamper-proof online voting**, reducing fraud and increasing election transparency.

Voter anonymity – Protects voter identity while ensuring integrity.

Automatic vote counting – Eliminates the need for manual vote counting and reduces errors.

5. Real Estate and Legal Agreements

Smart contracts simplify **property transactions** and enforce **legal agreements** without intermediaries.

Automated property transfers – Ownership changes are recorded on the blockchain once conditions are met.

Escrow services – Funds are released automatically once contract terms are fulfilled.

How Smart Contracts Are Deployed and Executed

1. Writing the Contract

Smart contracts are written in **blockchain-specific programming languages**. Some popular languages include:

Solidity (Ethereum and Binance Smart Chain)

Rust (Solana, Polkadot, NEAR)

Vyper (Ethereum alternative to Solidity)

2. Compiling the Contract

After writing the code, the smart contract is compiled into **bytecode**, which the blockchain can understand.

3. Deploying the Contract

The contract is then deployed to the blockchain using a **deployment transaction**. Once deployed, the contract gets a **unique address**, which users can interact with.

4. Interacting with the Contract

Users interact with smart contracts by sending **transactions** that trigger contract functions. These transactions are recorded on the blockchain, ensuring transparency and immutability.

For example, a user might call a **"sendTokens"** function to transfer funds, and the contract will **update balances accordingly**.

Limitations and Risks of Smart Contracts

Despite their advantages, smart contracts are **not without challenges**. Developers must carefully consider the following risks:

1. Security Vulnerabilities

Smart contracts are **immutable** once deployed, meaning that **bugs and vulnerabilities cannot be fixed**. If a contract contains a flaw, hackers can exploit it, leading to **loss of funds or security breaches**.

For example, the infamous **DAO Hack (2016)** on Ethereum resulted in **$60 million in stolen funds** due to a reentrancy bug in the contract's code.

How to mitigate security risks:

Conduct thorough testing before deployment.

Use formal verification to mathematically prove correctness.

Implement upgradeable smart contracts (where possible).

Follow best practices to prevent common exploits, such as reentrancy attacks and integer overflows.

2. High Gas Fees

Smart contract execution requires **computational power**, which translates into **gas fees** on networks like Ethereum. When the network is congested, fees can become prohibitively high.

Solutions to reduce costs:

Use **Layer 2 scaling solutions** (e.g., Optimistic Rollups, zk-Rollups).

Deploy contracts on **low-fee blockchains** (e.g., Solana, NEAR).

3. Legal and Regulatory Challenges

Since smart contracts operate **without centralized control**, they raise legal questions:

Are smart contracts legally binding agreements?

Who is responsible if a smart contract **fails or is exploited**?

How do governments regulate decentralized systems?

While blockchain technology challenges traditional legal structures, some jurisdictions are adapting **laws to recognize smart contracts** as enforceable agreements.

The Future of Smart Contracts

Smart contracts are revolutionizing **finance, commerce, governance, and digital ownership**. As blockchain technology evolves, we can expect:

More efficient contract execution through faster blockchain consensus mechanisms.

Lower transaction fees with advancements in scaling solutions.

Wider adoption as businesses integrate smart contracts into daily operations.

Improved security standards to prevent vulnerabilities and hacks.

By **understanding smart contracts** and their potential, developers and businesses can **build decentralized applications that are secure, transparent, and globally accessible**.

Smart contracts eliminate **trust barriers** and enable **automated, decentralized applications** that operate **without intermediaries**. They bring **transparency, security, and efficiency** to industries ranging from **finance to supply chain management**.

By leveraging **Rust-based smart contract frameworks**, developers can build **high-performance, scalable, and secure blockchain applications**, unlocking the full potential of decentralized technologies.

Overview of Rust-Based Smart Contract Frameworks

Blockchain development has evolved beyond simple transactions and now supports complex, self-executing programs known as **smart contracts**. These contracts automate processes without intermediaries, ensuring trustless execution. While **Solidity** dominates the Ethereum ecosystem, **Rust** has gained popularity for smart contract development due to its **performance, memory safety, and strict type system**.

Several blockchain platforms have adopted Rust as their primary language for smart contracts. The most widely used Rust-based smart contract frameworks include **Ink! (for Polkadot), Solana, and NEAR Protocol**. Each framework has unique features, execution models, and use cases. Understanding these differences is essential for choosing the right platform for a decentralized application (DApp) or blockchain project.

Ink! – Smart Contracts for Polkadot and Substrate

Ink! is a **smart contract framework built for the Polkadot ecosystem**. It is designed to work seamlessly with **Substrate**, the framework used to develop custom blockchains on Polkadot and Kusama. Ink! enables developers to write smart contracts in Rust and compile them into **WebAssembly (Wasm)** for execution on Substrate-based chains.

Why Ink!?

Ink! is specifically optimized for **Substrate blockchains**, making it an excellent choice for projects that require customizable blockchain logic. The **Wasm-based execution** model ensures that contracts run efficiently and securely without consuming excessive resources.

Ink! is ideal for building:

Decentralized finance (DeFi) applications on Polkadot parachains.

Custom smart contract platforms that operate within Substrate-based blockchains.

Enterprise solutions that require a flexible and scalable blockchain infrastructure.

Setting Up an Ink! Smart Contract

To develop smart contracts with Ink!, first install the required dependencies:

```
cargo install cargo-contract --force
rustup target add wasm32-unknown-unknown
```

Then, create a new Ink! project:

```
cargo contract new my_contract
cd my_contract
```

This generates a basic Ink! contract template. The main contract logic resides in `src/lib.rs`.

Writing a Basic Ink! Smart Contract

Below is an example of a **simple smart contract** that stores and updates a value.

```
#![cfg_attr(not(feature = "std"), no_std)]

use ink::prelude::*;
use ink::storage;

#[ink::contract]
mod my_contract {
    #[ink(storage)]
    pub struct MyContract {
        value: u32,
    }

    impl MyContract {
        #[ink(constructor)]
        pub fn new(init_value: u32) -> Self {
            Self { value: init_value }
        }

        #[ink(message)]
        pub fn set_value(&mut self, new_value: u32)
{
            self.value = new_value;
```

```
        }

        #[ink(message)]
        pub fn get_value(&self) -> u32 {
            self.value
        }
    }
}
```

This contract has:

A constructor (new) that initializes the contract with a value.

A setter function (set_value) to update the value.

A getter function (get_value) to retrieve the stored value.

To compile the contract into WebAssembly, run:

```
cargo contract build
```

And to deploy it on a Substrate-based blockchain:

```
cargo contract instantiate --args 100
```

Ink! smart contracts are efficient, secure, and seamlessly integrate with the **Polkadot and Kusama ecosystems**.

Solana – High-Performance Smart Contracts

Solana is a **high-speed blockchain** that supports smart contracts written in Rust and compiled directly into **machine code**. Unlike Ethereum's **EVM (Ethereum Virtual Machine)** or Polkadot's **Wasm execution**, Solana runs smart contracts as **on-chain programs** that interact with accounts in a unique execution model.

Why Solana?

Solana is optimized for **high-performance decentralized applications**, making it ideal for:

Decentralized finance (DeFi) platforms that require low latency and high throughput.

NFT marketplaces with instant transaction finality.

Gaming and metaverse applications needing real-time interactions.

How Solana Smart Contracts Work

Solana smart contracts are called **programs** and differ from Ethereum-based contracts in several ways:

Programs are stateless – they do not store persistent data. Instead, data is stored in accounts.

High-speed execution – transactions are processed in parallel using Solana's **Sealevel runtime**.

Low transaction costs – Solana can handle thousands of transactions per second at minimal fees.

Writing a Solana Smart Contract in Rust

To begin, install the Solana CLI and Rust development tools:

```
sh -c "$(curl -sSfL
https://release.solana.com/stable/install)"
cargo install --git https://github.com/solana-
labs/solana-program-library.git solana-cli
```

Next, create a new Solana smart contract:

```
cargo new --lib my_solana_contract
cd my_solana_contract
```

Edit `src/lib.rs` to define the contract logic:

```
use solana_program::{
    account_info::{next_account_info, AccountInfo},
    entrypoint,
    entrypoint::ProgramResult,
    pubkey::Pubkey,
};

entrypoint!(process_instruction);

fn process_instruction(
    _program_id: &Pubkey,
    accounts: &[AccountInfo],
```

```
        _instruction_data: &[u8],
) -> ProgramResult {
    let accounts_iter = &mut accounts.iter();
    let account =
next_account_info(accounts_iter)?;

    **account.lamports.borrow_mut() += 1000; //
Example logic
    Ok(())
}
```

This contract:

Defines an **entrypoint** (`process_instruction`) that gets called when a transaction interacts with the contract.

Modifies the **account balance** by adding 1000 lamports (Solana's smallest unit).

Solana contracts require careful **resource management** since they execute **directly on the blockchain without a virtual machine**.

NEAR Protocol – Developer-Friendly Smart Contracts

NEAR is a **scalable, developer-friendly blockchain** that supports smart contracts written in **Rust and AssemblyScript**. It uses **sharding technology** to improve transaction throughput and reduce costs.

Why NEAR?

NEAR is well-suited for:

Web3 applications that require easy onboarding for new users.

Low-cost transactions, making it ideal for microtransactions.

Decentralized identity and storage solutions.

Writing a NEAR Smart Contract in Rust

To start developing on NEAR, install the NEAR CLI:

```
npm install -g near-cli
```

Create a Rust-based NEAR smart contract:

```
cargo new --lib my_near_contract
cd my_near_contract
```

Edit `src/lib.rs` to define the contract logic:

```
use near_sdk::near_bindgen;

#[near_bindgen]
#[derive(Default)]
pub struct Counter {
    count: i32,
}

#[near_bindgen]
impl Counter {
    pub fn increment(&mut self) {
        self.count += 1;
    }

    pub fn get_count(&self) -> i32 {
        self.count
    }
}
```

This contract defines a simple **counter** that can be incremented and retrieved.

To compile the contract for NEAR's WebAssembly runtime:

```
cargo build --target wasm32-unknown-unknown --release
```

Deploy it using:

```
near deploy --accountId myaccount.testnet --wasmFile target/wasm32-unknown-unknown/release/my_near_contract.wasm
```

NEAR's focus on **usability and low fees** makes it an attractive choice for **consumer-facing applications**.

Rust-based smart contract frameworks offer **security, performance, and scalability** across different blockchain ecosystems. Ink! is best for **custom Polkadot blockchains**, Solana is optimized for **high-speed applications**, and NEAR provides a **user-friendly development experience**.

88

Choosing the right framework depends on **project requirements**, such as transaction speed, scalability, and security needs. By leveraging Rust's powerful features, developers can build **next-generation decentralized applications** with confidence.

Setting Up a Smart Contract Project

Smart contracts power decentralized applications by executing predefined logic on a blockchain. Writing a smart contract in **Rust** requires choosing the right blockchain framework, setting up the development environment, and understanding how smart contract execution works on different platforms.

Whether you're developing for **Polkadot (Ink!), Solana, or NEAR**, each blockchain has specific requirements for writing, compiling, and deploying smart contracts. Setting up a smart contract project properly ensures that your code runs efficiently, is secure, and meets the needs of the blockchain ecosystem you are building on.

This section provides a **detailed, step-by-step guide** to setting up a Rust-based smart contract project, covering **tool installation, project initialization, and contract deployment** on different blockchain platforms.

Choosing a Rust-Based Smart Contract Framework

Before setting up a smart contract project, you need to determine which blockchain platform you'll be developing on. Rust is used for smart contracts on several major platforms, each with its **own execution model and contract lifecycle**.

Ink! (for Polkadot and Substrate-based chains) – Uses **WebAssembly (Wasm)** to execute contracts on Substrate-based blockchains.

Solana (Rust-based on-chain programs) – Compiles smart contracts into **native machine code** for high-speed execution.

NEAR Protocol (Wasm-based execution) – Offers a **developer-friendly** environment with low fees and scalable infrastructure.

89

Each of these frameworks has its own tooling and setup process, but all require **Rust and its package manager, Cargo**.

Setting Up an Ink! Smart Contract Project (For Polkadot & Substrate)

Ink! is the primary Rust framework for writing **smart contracts on Polkadot and Substrate-based chains**. It compiles Rust code into **WebAssembly (Wasm)**, allowing efficient contract execution across multiple blockchain networks.

1. Installing Ink! Development Tools

Before you start, ensure that you have Rust installed. If Rust is not installed, install it using **Rustup**:

```
curl --proto '=https' --tlsv1.2 -sSf
https://sh.rustup.rs | sh
```

Once Rust is installed, add the **WebAssembly target** required for smart contract compilation:

```
rustup target add wasm32-unknown-unknown
```

Next, install the **cargo-contract** tool, which helps manage Ink! smart contract projects:

```
cargo install cargo-contract --force
```

This command installs the Ink! contract development tool and ensures that your Rust toolchain is up to date.

2. Creating a New Ink! Smart Contract Project

To create a new smart contract project, use the `cargo contract new` command:

```
cargo contract new my_contract
cd my_contract
```

This generates a template project with the following structure:

```
my_contract/
|— src/
|    ├— lib.rs  // Main smart contract logic
```

90

```
|— Cargo.toml  // Dependencies and project
metadata

|— tests/       // Unit tests for the contract
```

3. Writing a Basic Ink! Smart Contract

The main contract logic is written in **src/lib.rs**. Here's an example of a simple contract that stores a value:

```
#![cfg_attr(not(feature = "std"), no_std)]

use ink::prelude::*;
use ink::storage;

#[ink::contract]
mod my_contract {
    #[ink(storage)]
    pub struct MyContract {
        value: u32,
    }

    impl MyContract {
        #[ink(constructor)]
        pub fn new(init_value: u32) -> Self {
            Self { value: init_value }
        }

        #[ink(message)]
        pub fn set_value(&mut self, new_value: u32)
{
            self.value = new_value;
        }

        #[ink(message)]
        pub fn get_value(&self) -> u32 {
            self.value
        }
    }
}
```

4. Compiling and Deploying the Contract

To compile the contract into a Wasm binary, run:

```
cargo contract build
```
Once compiled, you can deploy the contract to a local or testnet Substrate-based blockchain using:

```
cargo contract instantiate --args 100
```
This deploys the contract with an initial value of **100**, allowing users to interact with it using the contract's `set_value` and `get_value` functions.

Setting Up a Solana Smart Contract Project

Solana uses **Rust-based on-chain programs** that execute directly on its **Sealevel runtime**, optimizing performance for high-speed transactions. Unlike Ethereum's **EVM** or Polkadot's **Wasm execution**, Solana smart contracts interact with **accounts rather than storing state inside the contract**.

1. Installing Solana Development Tools

First, install the **Solana CLI**, which provides tools for interacting with the Solana blockchain:

```
sh -c "$(curl -sSfL
https://release.solana.com/stable/install)"
```
After installing the CLI, verify that the Solana development environment is correctly set up:

```
solana --version
```

2. Creating a New Solana Smart Contract Project

Create a new Rust-based **Solana program** (smart contract) using Cargo:

```
cargo new --lib my_solana_contract
cd my_solana_contract
```

3. Writing a Basic Solana Smart Contract

Edit the `src/lib.rs` file to define a simple Solana smart contract that transfers tokens between accounts:

```
use solana_program::{
    account_info::{next_account_info, AccountInfo},
    entrypoint,
    entrypoint::ProgramResult,
    pubkey::Pubkey,
```

```
};

entrypoint!(process_instruction);

fn process_instruction(
    _program_id: &Pubkey,
    accounts: &[AccountInfo],
    _instruction_data: &[u8],
) -> ProgramResult {
    let accounts_iter = &mut accounts.iter();
    let account =
next_account_info(accounts_iter)?;

    **account.lamports.borrow_mut() += 1000; //
Example logic to increase balance
    Ok(())
}
```

4. Compiling and Deploying the Contract

To compile the contract, run:

```
cargo build-bpf
```

Once compiled, deploy the contract using the **Solana CLI**:

```
solana program deploy
target/deploy/my_solana_contract.so
```

This uploads the contract to the Solana blockchain, allowing users to execute its logic by sending transactions.

Setting Up a NEAR Smart Contract Project

NEAR Protocol provides a **developer-friendly** Rust environment for building smart contracts, using **WebAssembly** as its execution model.

1. Installing NEAR Development Tools

Install the **NEAR CLI** to interact with the blockchain:

```
npm install -g near-cli
```

2. Creating a New NEAR Smart Contract Project

To start a NEAR smart contract project in Rust, create a new library project:

```
cargo new --lib my_near_contract
```

93

```
cd my_near_contract
```

3. Writing a Basic NEAR Smart Contract

Edit the `src/lib.rs` file to define a simple contract that stores and updates a counter:

```
use near_sdk::near_bindgen;

#[near_bindgen]
#[derive(Default)]
pub struct Counter {
    count: i32,
}

#[near_bindgen]
impl Counter {
    pub fn increment(&mut self) {
        self.count += 1;
    }

    pub fn get_count(&self) -> i32 {
        self.count
    }
}
```

4. Compiling and Deploying the Contract

Compile the contract for WebAssembly execution:

```
cargo build --target wasm32-unknown-unknown --
release
```

Deploy the contract using the NEAR CLI:

```
near deploy --accountId myaccount.testnet --
wasmFile target/wasm32-unknown-
unknown/release/my_near_contract.wasm
```

This contract can now be interacted with on the NEAR blockchain.

Setting up a Rust-based smart contract project requires **installing the right tools, writing efficient code, and deploying the contract to the blockchain**. Whether you're building on **Polkadot (Ink!), Solana, or NEAR**, Rust provides **a secure, high-performance programming environment** for decentralized applications.

By following these steps, developers can **set up, compile, and deploy** smart contracts efficiently, ensuring seamless interaction with blockchain networks.

Chapter 5: Writing Secure Smart Contracts

Smart contracts handle **financial transactions, governance rules, and critical data**, making security a **top priority**. A single vulnerability in a smart contract can lead to **loss of funds, data manipulation, or even total system failure**.

While **Rust** offers strong memory safety guarantees, smart contract security goes beyond preventing **buffer overflows** or **null pointer dereferences**. It requires **careful handling of contract logic, access control, reentrancy protection, and state management** to avoid common vulnerabilities.

Common Security Vulnerabilities in Smart Contracts

Smart contracts are the backbone of decentralized applications. They **automate agreements, facilitate financial transactions, and enforce business logic** without intermediaries. However, once deployed on a blockchain, a smart contract **cannot be modified**, meaning any vulnerability in the code can be **exploited permanently**.

Over the years, many smart contracts have been hacked due to **reentrancy attacks, integer overflows, unchecked external calls, improper access controls, and logic errors**. These vulnerabilities have led to **massive financial losses** in the blockchain ecosystem.

While **Rust** provides strong memory safety and type checking, smart contract security extends beyond **avoiding buffer overflows**—it involves **carefully structuring contract logic to prevent unexpected behaviors**. This section covers the most common security vulnerabilities in smart contracts, their real-world impact, and how to mitigate them effectively.

Reentrancy Attacks: Exploiting External Calls

A **reentrancy attack** occurs when a contract calls an **external function** before updating its state, allowing a malicious contract to repeatedly withdraw funds **before the balance is updated**.

This is one of the most devastating attacks in blockchain history, responsible for the infamous **DAO hack (2016)** on Ethereum, where an attacker exploited a reentrancy vulnerability to drain **$60 million worth of ETH**.

How a Reentrancy Attack Works

Consider a **vulnerable Rust smart contract** that allows users to withdraw funds:

```
#[ink::contract]
mod vulnerable_contract {
    #[ink(storage)]
    pub struct VulnerableContract {
        balances: ink::storage::Mapping<AccountId,
Balance>,
    }

    impl VulnerableContract {
        #[ink(message)]
        pub fn deposit(&mut self) {
            let caller = self.env().caller();
            let balance =
self.balances.get(&caller).unwrap_or(0);
            self.balances.insert(&caller, &(balance
+ self.env().transferred_value()));
        }

        #[ink(message)]
        pub fn withdraw(&mut self, amount: Balance)
{
            let caller = self.env().caller();
            let balance =
self.balances.get(&caller).unwrap_or(0);
            assert!(balance >= amount,
"Insufficient balance");

            // Sends funds before updating balance
(Vulnerable!)
```

```
            self.env().transfer(caller,
amount).unwrap();

            // Updates balance after transferring
(Too late!)
            self.balances.insert(&caller, &(balance
- amount));
        }
    }
}
```

This contract has **two major problems**:

It **sends funds before updating the user's balance**.

It does not check **whether the external contract is calling recursively**.

How an Attacker Exploits This

The attacker **deposits** funds into the contract.

They deploy a **malicious contract** that overrides the `withdraw` function.

When `withdraw()` is called, their contract **calls `withdraw()` again recursively before the balance is updated**.

This process repeats until all funds are drained.

How to Prevent Reentrancy Attacks

To prevent this, **update state before sending funds**:

```
impl VulnerableContract {
    #[ink(message)]
    pub fn withdraw(&mut self, amount: Balance) {
        let caller = self.env().caller();
        let balance =
self.balances.get(&caller).unwrap_or(0);
        assert!(balance >= amount, "Insufficient
balance");

        // Update balance first (Prevents
reentrancy)
        self.balances.insert(&caller, &(balance -
amount));
```

```
        // Transfer funds after updating the
balance
        self.env().transfer(caller,
amount).unwrap();
    }
}
```

This simple **reordering of operations** neutralizes reentrancy attacks, making the contract significantly safer.

Integer Overflows and Underflows

Integer overflows occur when an arithmetic operation **exceeds the maximum value** a data type can hold. Similarly, **underflows** occur when a value **drops below zero**, leading to **unexpected behavior**.

While **Rust prevents overflow in debug mode**, WebAssembly (Wasm) execution may not enforce these checks, depending on the blockchain environment.

Example of Integer Overflow

```
fn add_balance(balance: u32, amount: u32) -> u32 {
    balance + amount // Can overflow if amount is
too large!
}
```

If `balance` is **close to u32::MAX**, adding `amount` could cause an **integer overflow**, leading to incorrect values being stored.

How an Attacker Exploits This

An attacker could **intentionally overflow** a value, causing:

Bypassing access control (e.g., setting their role to an admin).

Manipulating financial transactions (e.g., receiving more tokens than allowed).

How to Prevent Integer Overflows

99

Rust provides **safe arithmetic operations** using `checked_add()`, `checked_sub()`, and `checked_mul()`:

```
fn add_balance(balance: u32, amount: u32) -> Option<u32> {
    balance.checked_add(amount) // Returns None if overflow occurs
}
```

If an overflow is detected, the function **returns None**, preventing execution of unintended logic.

Unchecked External Calls

Smart contracts often **interact with external contracts** by calling their functions. If these external calls **fail or behave unexpectedly**, the calling contract might break or expose vulnerabilities.

Example of an Unchecked External Call

```
#[ink(message)]
pub fn send_funds(&self, recipient: AccountId,
amount: Balance) {
    self.env().transfer(recipient,
amount).unwrap(); // If this fails, contract
execution halts!
}
```

If the recipient contract **rejects the transfer** or **fails**, this function **will panic and halt execution**.

How an Attacker Exploits This

An attacker could deploy a **malicious contract** that **intentionally fails** when receiving funds, causing the sender's contract to break. This could be used to **block other transactions or manipulate contract logic**.

How to Prevent This

Always **handle failures explicitly**:

```
#[ink(message)]
pub fn safe_send_funds(&self, recipient: AccountId,
amount: Balance) -> bool {
```

```
match self.env().transfer(recipient, amount) {
    Ok(_) => true,  // Transfer succeeded
    Err(_) => false, // Handle failure safely
    }
}
```

By returning a **boolean result** instead of panicking, the contract can **handle errors gracefully**.

Improper Access Control

Many vulnerabilities stem from **poorly designed access control**, where **unauthorized users** gain access to sensitive contract functions.

Example of a Vulnerable Contract

```
#[ink(storage)]
pub struct UnsafeContract {
    owner: AccountId,
}

impl UnsafeContract {
    #[ink(message)]
    pub fn change_owner(&mut self, new_owner:
AccountId) {
        self.owner = new_owner; // No access
control!
    }
}
```

Here, **anyone** can call `change_owner()` and take control of the contract.

How to Prevent Unauthorized Access

Restrict sensitive functions to **authorized users only**:

```
#[ink(storage)]
pub struct SecureContract {
    owner: AccountId,
}

impl SecureContract {
    #[ink(constructor)]
    pub fn new() -> Self {
        Self {
```

```
        owner: Self::env().caller(),
        }
    }

    #[ink(message)]
    pub fn change_owner(&mut self, new_owner:
AccountId) {
        assert!(self.env().caller() == self.owner,
"Not authorized!");
        self.owner = new_owner;
    }
}
```

This ensures that **only the contract owner** can modify ownership, preventing unauthorized takeovers.

Security vulnerabilities in smart contracts can **lead to massive financial losses and system failures**. By understanding these risks and implementing **safe coding practices**, developers can **build more secure and reliable blockchain applications**.

The key takeaways for writing **secure Rust smart contracts**:

Prevent reentrancy attacks by **updating state before transferring funds**.

Use checked arithmetic to **avoid integer overflows and underflows**.

Handle external calls safely to **avoid unexpected failures**.

Enforce proper access control to **restrict sensitive functions**.

Security should be a **core principle in smart contract development**—not an afterthought. Every function must be **carefully designed and tested** to prevent **exploits that can compromise an entire blockchain ecosystem**.

Best Practices for Safe Rust Smart Contracts

Security is critical in smart contract development. Unlike traditional applications, **smart contracts are immutable once deployed**, meaning any vulnerability in the code remains permanently exploitable. A single bug can lead to **financial loss, network disruption, or a complete contract takeover**.

Rust provides **memory safety, type safety, and strict compiler checks**, reducing many security risks present in other languages. However, writing secure smart contracts requires **thoughtful design, structured execution flow, and defensive programming practices**.

This section explores **best practices for writing safe Rust smart contracts**, covering **secure state management, proper access control, safe external calls, and defensive coding techniques** to prevent exploits.

1. Enforce Proper Access Control

Smart contracts often include **administrative functions** that modify contract behavior, change ownership, or update parameters. If these functions are not **properly restricted**, unauthorized users can **modify the contract state** and gain control.

Example of Poor Access Control

```
#[ink(storage)]
pub struct UnsafeContract {
    owner: AccountId,
}

impl UnsafeContract {
    #[ink(message)]
    pub fn change_owner(&mut self, new_owner:
AccountId) {
        self.owner = new_owner; // No access
control!
    }
}
```

In this contract, **anyone** can call `change_owner()` and take ownership, leading to a **complete contract takeover**.

How to Secure It

Restrict **sensitive functions** to authorized users using an **ownership check**:

```
#[ink(storage)]
pub struct SecureContract {
    owner: AccountId,
}
```

```
impl SecureContract {
    #[ink(constructor)]
    pub fn new() -> Self {
        Self {
            owner: Self::env().caller(),
        }
    }

    #[ink(message)]
    pub fn change_owner(&mut self, new_owner:
AccountId) {
        assert!(self.env().caller() == self.owner,
"Not authorized!");
        self.owner = new_owner;
    }
}
```

With this check, **only the contract owner** can call `change_owner()`, preventing unauthorized access.

Using Role-Based Access Control

For more complex applications, **role-based access control (RBAC)** ensures different permissions for different users. Instead of a single owner, you can assign **multiple roles**:

```
#[ink(storage)]
pub struct RoleBasedContract {
    admins: ink::storage::Mapping<AccountId, bool>,
}

impl RoleBasedContract {
    #[ink(constructor)]
    pub fn new(admin: AccountId) -> Self {
        let mut admins =
ink::storage::Mapping::new();
        admins.insert(&admin, &true);
        Self { admins }
    }

    #[ink(message)]
    pub fn add_admin(&mut self, new_admin:
AccountId) {
```

104

```
assert!(self.admins.get(&self.env().caller()).unwra
p_or(false), "Not an admin!");
        self.admins.insert(&new_admin, &true);
    }
}
```

This ensures **only existing admins** can add new ones, creating a **more flexible access control model**.

2. Prevent Reentrancy Attacks

A **reentrancy attack** occurs when a contract calls an external contract before **updating its state**, allowing the external contract to call back into the original function **before the first call is completed**. This can **drain funds before the contract realizes it**.

Example of a Reentrancy Vulnerability

```
#[ink(message)]
pub fn withdraw(&mut self, amount: Balance) {
    let caller = self.env().caller();
    let balance =
self.balances.get(&caller).unwrap_or(0);

    assert!(balance >= amount, "Insufficient
funds");

    // Sends funds before updating balance
(Vulnerable)
    self.env().transfer(caller, amount).unwrap();

    // Updates balance after transferring (Too
late!)
    self.balances.insert(&caller, &(balance -
amount));
}
```

An attacker can **exploit this** by creating a contract that **recursively calls** `withdraw()`, repeatedly draining funds before the balance updates.

How to Secure It

The correct way to **prevent reentrancy** is to **update the contract state before making external calls**:

```
#[ink(message)]
pub fn withdraw(&mut self, amount: Balance) {
    let caller = self.env().caller();
    let balance =
self.balances.get(&caller).unwrap_or(0);

    assert!(balance >= amount, "Insufficient
funds");

    // Update balance first (Prevents reentrancy)
    self.balances.insert(&caller, &(balance -
amount));

    // Transfer funds only after updating balance
    self.env().transfer(caller, amount).unwrap();
}
```

This **eliminates reentrancy risks** by ensuring that no external call can interfere with state updates.

3. Use Safe Arithmetic Operations

Integer overflows and underflows can lead to **incorrect values, broken logic, or contract exploits**.

Example of Integer Overflow

```
fn add_balance(balance: u32, amount: u32) -> u32 {
    balance + amount // Can overflow if amount is
too large!
}
```

If balance is near u32::MAX, adding amount will **wrap around**, creating an incorrect balance.

How to Prevent This

Rust provides **checked arithmetic functions** that prevent overflows and underflows:

```
fn add_balance(balance: u32, amount: u32) ->
Option<u32> {
```

106

```
    balance.checked_add(amount) // Returns None if
overflow occurs
}
```

By using `checked_add()`, `checked_sub()`, and `checked_mul()`, the contract **explicitly handles arithmetic failures**, preventing unexpected behavior.

4. Handle External Calls Safely

Smart contracts **interact with other contracts**, but if an external call **fails or behaves unexpectedly**, the calling contract can break.

Example of an Unchecked External Call

```
#[ink(message)]
pub fn send_funds(&self, recipient: AccountId,
amount: Balance) {
    self.env().transfer(recipient,
amount).unwrap(); // If this fails, contract
execution halts!
}
```

If `recipient` is a **malicious contract** that intentionally fails, it can **prevent transactions from being completed**.

How to Secure It

Handle external call failures gracefully by **using error handling**:

```
#[ink(message)]
pub fn safe_send_funds(&self, recipient: AccountId,
amount: Balance) -> bool {
    match self.env().transfer(recipient, amount) {
        Ok(_) => true,  // Transfer succeeded
        Err(_) => false, // Handle failure safely
    }
}
```

This ensures **a failing transaction does not disrupt the entire contract**, making the contract more resilient.

5. Implement Event Logging for Transparency

Smart contracts should log **important actions** such as **fund transfers, role changes, and state updates**. This helps with **troubleshooting and auditing**.

Example of Event Logging

```
#[ink(event)]
pub struct FundsTransferred {
    #[ink(topic)]
    from: AccountId,
    #[ink(topic)]
    to: AccountId,
    amount: Balance,
}

#[ink(message)]
pub fn transfer(&mut self, recipient: AccountId,
amount: Balance) {
    let caller = self.env().caller();
    self.env().emit_event(FundsTransferred { from:
caller, to: recipient, amount });

    self.env().transfer(recipient,
amount).unwrap();
}
```

Events help **track transactions**, making it easier to detect **suspicious activity**.

Writing safe Rust smart contracts requires **careful execution flow, defensive coding, and explicit security checks**.

The key principles for secure contracts:

Restrict access to sensitive functions using **proper ownership and role-based access control**.

Prevent reentrancy attacks by **updating contract state before making external calls**.

Use safe arithmetic functions to **avoid integer overflows and underflows**.

Handle external call failures explicitly, ensuring that a single failed transaction does not break contract logic.

Log important events for **better debugging and security monitoring**.

By following these best practices, developers can **minimize security risks** and build **trustworthy, efficient, and attack-resistant** smart contracts. Security must always be a **top priority** in blockchain development.

Testing and Debugging Smart Contracts

Smart contracts are **immutable** once deployed, meaning **bugs cannot be fixed after launch**. Unlike traditional software, where patches and updates are routine, smart contracts require **rigorous testing before deployment** to ensure they function correctly and securely.

Testing helps identify **logical errors, security vulnerabilities, and edge cases** before a contract interacts with real assets. Debugging, on the other hand, allows developers to **trace issues, analyze contract behavior, and resolve unexpected failures** during development.

A well-tested smart contract **reduces risks, builds trust, and ensures smooth operation** on the blockchain. This section covers **testing strategies, debugging tools, and real-world techniques** for ensuring Rust smart contracts are secure and function as intended.

Why Testing is Critical for Smart Contracts

In traditional applications, **bugs can be fixed with updates**, but in smart contracts, a **single vulnerability can permanently lock funds, allow unauthorized withdrawals, or disrupt an entire network**.

Testing ensures:

Correct execution of contract logic, ensuring all functions behave as expected.

Security vulnerabilities are identified and fixed before deployment.

Edge cases are handled properly, preventing unexpected failures.

Gas efficiency is optimized, reducing execution costs.

Skipping proper testing can **lead to catastrophic failures**. Many high-profile hacks, such as **The DAO hack** and **Parity's frozen funds incident**, could have been prevented with thorough testing.

Unit Testing in Rust Smart Contracts

Rust has a **built-in test framework** that allows developers to **test individual contract functions** in isolation. Unit tests help verify that **each function produces the expected output** given different inputs.

Setting Up Unit Tests

Unit tests are written **inside the contract file** or in a separate `tests` directory.

Example: Testing a Simple Ink! Smart Contract

This contract stores a value and allows users to update it.

```
#[ink::contract]
mod my_contract {
    #[ink(storage)]
    pub struct MyContract {
        value: u32,
    }

    impl MyContract {
        #[ink(constructor)]
        pub fn new(init_value: u32) -> Self {
            Self { value: init_value }
        }

        #[ink(message)]
        pub fn set_value(&mut self, new_value: u32)
{
            self.value = new_value;
        }

        #[ink(message)]
        pub fn get_value(&self) -> u32 {
            self.value
        }
    }
}
```

Writing Unit Tests

```rust
#[cfg(test)]
mod tests {
    use super::*;

    #[test]
    fn test_initial_value() {
        let contract = MyContract::new(100);
        assert_eq!(contract.get_value(), 100);
    }

    #[test]
    fn test_set_value() {
        let mut contract = MyContract::new(100);
        contract.set_value(200);
        assert_eq!(contract.get_value(), 200);
    }
}
```

Running Unit Tests

Run unit tests using Cargo:

```
cargo test
```

If all tests pass, it confirms the contract's **basic logic is functioning correctly**. If a test fails, Rust will display **the exact line where the error occurred**, helping debug the issue.

Integration Testing for Smart Contracts

While unit tests check **individual functions**, integration tests ensure that **different parts of the contract work together correctly**.

Example: Testing Contract Interactions

Let's test a contract where multiple users deposit and withdraw funds.

```rust
#[cfg(test)]
mod tests {
    use super::*;
```

111

```rust
#[test]
fn test_deposit_and_withdraw() {
    let mut contract = MyContract::new();

    // Simulate user deposits
    contract.deposit(100);
    assert_eq!(contract.get_balance(), 100);

    // Simulate user withdrawal
    contract.withdraw(50);
    assert_eq!(contract.get_balance(), 50);
}
}
```

Simulating Multiple Users

To test contract interactions **from different users**, use Rust's **account simulation tools**:

```rust
#[test]
fn test_multiple_users() {
    let mut contract = MyContract::new();

    let alice = AccountId::from([0x01; 32]);
    let bob = AccountId::from([0x02; 32]);

    contract.deposit_for(alice, 100);
    contract.deposit_for(bob, 50);

    assert_eq!(contract.get_balance(alice), 100);
    assert_eq!(contract.get_balance(bob), 50);
}
```

This ensures the contract correctly **tracks balances for different users**.

Debugging Smart Contracts

Debugging helps **identify errors, unexpected behaviors, and performance bottlenecks**. Since smart contracts run on **blockchains, debugging them requires specialized tools**.

Using Logging for Debugging

Rust's smart contract frameworks, like **Ink! and Solana**, allow **event logging**, which provides **real-time feedback on contract execution**.

Example: Adding Logging in Ink!

```
#[ink(event)]
pub struct ValueChanged {
    #[ink(topic)]
    previous: u32,
    #[ink(topic)]
    new: u32,
}

#[ink(message)]
pub fn set_value(&mut self, new_value: u32) {
    let old_value = self.value;
    self.value = new_value;

    self.env().emit_event(ValueChanged {
        previous: old_value,
        new: new_value,
    });
}
```

Now, whenever `set_value()` is called, an event is **logged on the blockchain**, making it easier to **track changes**.

Debugging with Print Statements (Solana)

Solana programs do not support **standard Rust debugging tools** because they run in a constrained environment. However, developers can use **print statements** for debugging:

```
msg!("Transaction executed successfully, new balance: {}", balance);
```

To view logs from a Solana smart contract:

```
solana logs
```

Running Local Blockchain Simulations

Before deploying on a live blockchain, test your contract in a **local environment**.

Using Substrate's Ink! Playground

113

For Ink! contracts, you can use the **Substrate Contracts Playground** to **deploy and interact with your contract in a sandboxed environment**.

```
cargo contract instantiate --args 100
```
This deploys the contract on a local node, allowing you to **test it without real tokens**.

Using Solana Test Validator

For Solana, the **test validator** allows running a **private blockchain instance**:

```
solana-test-validator
```
To deploy and test a contract locally:

```
solana program deploy my_solana_program.so
```

Fuzz Testing: Detecting Edge Cases

Fuzz testing **randomly generates inputs** to test for unexpected failures. This is useful for **finding vulnerabilities in smart contracts**.

Example: Fuzz Testing in Rust

Install **cargo-fuzz**:

```
cargo install cargo-fuzz
```
Run a fuzz test:

```
cargo fuzz run my_fuzz_target
```
This helps detect **integer overflows, logic errors, and edge case failures**.

Security Audits

Even after extensive testing, **manual and automated security audits** are essential to **ensure no vulnerabilities remain**.

Automated Tools for Smart Contract Audits

Cargo Clippy – Detects potential inefficiencies and security risks in Rust code.

Cargo Audit – Scans for dependencies with known vulnerabilities.

Run security checks with:

114

```
cargo clippy --all-targets
cargo audit
```

Manual Code Reviews

A smart contract should **undergo peer review by security experts** before deployment. Reviewing code manually **catches logical errors** that automated tools might miss.

Testing and debugging are essential to **ensuring the security and reliability of smart contracts**. By following structured testing practices, using debugging tools effectively, and conducting thorough audits, developers can **prevent costly mistakes and build trust in decentralized applications**.

Smart contract security is **not just about writing good code**—it's about **continuously testing, refining, and ensuring every function performs exactly as expected**.

Chapter 6: Deploying Smart Contracts

Writing a smart contract is just the beginning. To make it **accessible and functional on a blockchain**, it must be **compiled, deployed, and optimized** for efficiency. Once deployed, users and decentralized applications (DApps) can interact with the contract using **Web3 libraries**.

Smart contract deployment involves **preparing the contract for execution, minimizing gas costs, and ensuring smooth interaction** with blockchain clients.

Compiling and Deploying Rust Smart Contracts

Smart contracts written in Rust power **decentralized applications (DApps)** across multiple blockchain networks, including **Polkadot (Ink!), Solana, and NEAR**. These contracts must be **compiled into executable formats** that are compatible with their respective blockchain environments before they can be deployed and interacted with.

Since different blockchain platforms have unique **execution models**, the compilation and deployment process varies. **Ink! contracts** are compiled to **WebAssembly (Wasm)**, **Solana contracts** are compiled into **native machine code**, and **NEAR contracts** also use **Wasm** but with a different runtime structure.

Compiling and Deploying an Ink! Smart Contract (For Polkadot & Substrate Chains)

Ink! is the **Rust-based smart contract framework** for Substrate, the blockchain development framework used by Polkadot, Kusama, and other networks. Ink! smart contracts **run on WebAssembly (Wasm)** and are deployed to a **Substrate node**.

Step 1: Installing the Required Tools

Before compiling an Ink! contract, ensure that **Rust and its toolchain** are installed. If Rust is not installed, install it using Rustup:

```
curl --proto '=https' --tlsv1.2 -sSf
https://sh.rustup.rs | sh
```

Next, install the **WebAssembly target**, which is required for compiling smart contracts:

```
rustup target add wasm32-unknown-unknown
```

Finally, install the **cargo-contract** tool, which helps compile and deploy Ink! contracts:

```
cargo install cargo-contract --force
```

Step 2: Writing an Ink! Smart Contract

An Ink! contract is structured similarly to a Rust program but with **blockchain-specific logic**. Below is a simple smart contract that **stores and updates a value**:

```
#![cfg_attr(not(feature = "std"), no_std)]

use ink::prelude::*;
use ink::storage;

#[ink::contract]
mod my_contract {
    #[ink(storage)]
    pub struct MyContract {
        value: u32,
    }

    impl MyContract {
        #[ink(constructor)]
        pub fn new(init_value: u32) -> Self {
            Self { value: init_value }
        }

        #[ink(message)]
        pub fn set_value(&mut self, new_value: u32)
{
            self.value = new_value;
        }
```

```
        #[ink(message)]
        pub fn get_value(&self) -> u32 {
            self.value
        }
    }
}
```

Step 3: Compiling the Ink! Smart Contract

Navigate to the contract directory and build the contract:

```
cargo contract build
```

This command compiles the contract into a **WebAssembly (.wasm) binary**, ready for deployment. The output will include:

`my_contract.wasm` – The compiled contract file.

`my_contract.contract` – A bundled contract file containing metadata.

Step 4: Deploying the Contract on a Local Substrate Node

To deploy and test the contract, **run a local Substrate node**:

```
substrate-contracts-node --dev
```

Then deploy the contract using:

```
cargo contract instantiate --args 100
```

This deploys the contract and initializes the stored value to **100**.

To interact with the deployed contract, use the **Polkadot.js Apps UI**, which allows calling contract functions from a web interface.

Compiling and Deploying a Solana Smart Contract

Solana's smart contracts, called **on-chain programs**, differ from traditional contracts because they **do not store persistent state within the contract itself**. Instead, state is stored in **separate accounts**, making Solana **highly scalable and efficient**.

Step 1: Installing Solana Development Tools

First, install the **Solana CLI**, which is used to compile, deploy, and interact with smart contracts:

118

```
sh -c "$(curl -sSfL
https://release.solana.com/stable/install)"
```
After installation, verify that the CLI is set up correctly:

```
solana --version
```

Step 2: Writing a Solana Smart Contract in Rust

A basic Solana smart contract **increments a stored counter** each time it is called:

```
use solana_program::{
    account_info::{next_account_info, AccountInfo},
    entrypoint,
    entrypoint::ProgramResult,
    pubkey::Pubkey,
    msg,
};

entrypoint!(process_instruction);

fn process_instruction(
    _program_id: &Pubkey,
    accounts: &[AccountInfo],
    _instruction_data: &[u8],
) -> ProgramResult {
    let accounts_iter = &mut accounts.iter();
    let account =
next_account_info(accounts_iter)?;

    **account.lamports.borrow_mut() += 1000; //
Example logic

    msg!("Funds added to account");
    Ok(())
}
```

Step 3: Compiling the Solana Smart Contract

Navigate to the contract directory and compile it using **Solana's BPF toolchain**:

```
cargo build-bpf
```
This generates a .so file, which is **the compiled Solana program**.

119

Step 4: Deploying the Contract to a Local Solana Node

Start a **local Solana validator** to test the contract before deploying to the mainnet:

solana-test-validator

Deploy the compiled contract:

```
solana program deploy
target/deploy/my_solana_contract.so
```

This returns a **program ID**, which is needed to interact with the contract.

To call the contract from a frontend application, use **Solana Web3 libraries**.

Compiling and Deploying a NEAR Smart Contract

NEAR contracts execute in **WebAssembly**, similar to Ink! but with a different runtime. NEAR also **uses human-readable account names** instead of cryptographic addresses.

Step 1: Installing NEAR Development Tools

Install the NEAR CLI to deploy and interact with contracts:

```
npm install -g near-cli
```

Step 2: Writing a Simple NEAR Smart Contract in Rust

A basic contract that **stores a counter**:

```
use near_sdk::near_bindgen;

#[near_bindgen]
#[derive(Default)]
pub struct Counter {
    count: i32,
}

#[near_bindgen]
impl Counter {
    pub fn increment(&mut self) {
        self.count += 1;
    }
```

```
    pub fn get_count(&self) -> i32 {
        self.count
    }
}
```

Step 3: Compiling the Contract for NEAR

Compile the contract to WebAssembly:

```
cargo build --target wasm32-unknown-unknown --release
```

Step 4: Deploying the Contract to NEAR Testnet

Deploy using NEAR CLI:

```
near deploy --accountId mycontract.testnet --wasmFile target/wasm32-unknown-unknown/release/my_near_contract.wasm
```

This makes the contract available on **NEAR's testnet**.

Compiling and deploying Rust smart contracts depends on **the blockchain platform**:

Ink! contracts compile to **Wasm and deploy** to **Substrate-based blockchains**.

Solana contracts compile to **native machine code** and deploy as **on-chain programs**.

NEAR contracts use **Wasm with NEAR's runtime** for execution.

By following these **step-by-step processes**, developers can **successfully deploy Rust-based smart contracts** and ensure they function correctly in a **decentralized environment**.

Gas Optimization and Performance Considerations

Deploying a smart contract to a blockchain is only the beginning. Once deployed, every interaction with the contract **consumes computational resources**, which results in **gas fees**. These fees vary depending on the blockchain, the complexity of the operation, and network congestion.

Gas optimization is critical because **lowering gas costs makes contracts more efficient, scalable, and affordable for users**. A well-optimized contract **reduces unnecessary computations, minimizes storage usage, and executes transactions efficiently**.

Every blockchain **charges fees** for executing smart contracts. These fees cover:

Computation – The cost of running contract logic and calculations.

Storage – The cost of storing data on-chain.

Transaction Size – The cost of sending data to the blockchain.

If a contract is inefficient, **users pay higher transaction fees**, and operations may take longer to execute. Optimizing gas usage ensures that **contracts remain cost-effective and scalable**.

Gas Optimization in Ink! Smart Contracts (Polkadot & Substrate)

Ink! contracts run on **Substrate-based blockchains** and execute in a **WebAssembly (Wasm) environment**. Since Wasm-based execution charges fees for **computations and storage**, efficient contract design is crucial.

Minimizing Storage Usage

Storing data **on-chain** is expensive. Instead of using **vectors or lists** to store data, it is more gas-efficient to use **mapping structures**.

Example: Avoiding Expensive Vector Operations

A poorly optimized contract might store balances in a **vector**, requiring **iteration** to find a user's balance:

```
#[ink(storage)]
pub struct InefficientContract {
    balances: Vec<(AccountId, Balance)>,
}

impl InefficientContract {
    #[ink(message)]
```

```
    pub fn get_balance(&self, user: AccountId) ->
Balance {
        for (account, balance) in &self.balances {
            if *account == user {
                return *balance;
            }
        }
        0
    }
}
```

This approach **scales poorly** as the number of users grows, increasing gas costs due to the **linear search** operation.

Optimized Approach: Using Mapping

A more efficient method is to use **Mapping**, which allows **constant-time lookups**:

```
#[ink(storage)]
pub struct OptimizedContract {
    balances: ink::storage::Mapping<AccountId,
Balance>,
}

impl OptimizedContract {
    #[ink(message)]
    pub fn get_balance(&self, user: AccountId) ->
Balance {
        self.balances.get(&user).unwrap_or(0)
    }
}
```

This approach **eliminates iteration**, significantly reducing **gas consumption**.

Reducing Contract Deployment Costs

A contract's initial deployment **stores the contract logic on-chain**, which can be costly. To reduce this:

Use contract proxies – Deploy a minimal contract that references a **main contract**, reducing storage costs.

Remove unnecessary dependencies – Unused imports and functions **increase contract size**.

Use Rust's `cargo tree` to check dependencies:

```
cargo tree --depth 1
```

Removing unnecessary dependencies **reduces Wasm size and improves execution efficiency**.

Gas Optimization in Solana Smart Contracts

Solana is **designed for high throughput**, but smart contract execution still incurs costs based on **compute units (CU)**. Contracts that use excessive computation **consume more compute units**, leading to higher transaction fees.

Minimizing Compute Unit Consumption

Every operation in a Solana smart contract has an **associated compute cost**. Avoiding **expensive computations** ensures efficient execution.

Example: Avoiding Redundant Hashing Operations

An inefficient contract might **hash values multiple times**, unnecessarily consuming compute resources:

```rust
use solana_program::{
    program_pack::Pack,
    pubkey::Pubkey,
    msg,
};

fn process_instruction(data: &[u8]) ->
ProgramResult {
    let hashed_value = sha256::hash(data); //
Expensive operation
    let double_hashed =
sha256::hash(&hashed_value); // Avoid redundant
computations
    msg!("Final hash: {:?}", double_hashed);
    Ok(())
}
```

Optimized Approach: Compute Once and Reuse

Instead of hashing the same value multiple times, compute **once** and reuse the result:

```
fn process_instruction(data: &[u8]) ->
ProgramResult {
    let hashed_value = sha256::hash(data);
    msg!("Final hash: {:?}", hashed_value);
    Ok(())
}
```

This reduces **redundant computations**, saving **compute units and transaction fees**.

Optimizing Account Storage

In Solana, **accounts store contract state**, but storage is **limited and expensive**. Contracts should:

Use the smallest possible data structures to minimize on-chain storage.

Use PDA (Program Derived Addresses) to store state in program-controlled accounts.

Instead of storing a large struct, **store only essential fields**:

```
#[repr(C)]
#[derive(Clone, Debug, PartialEq)]
pub struct AccountData {
    pub balance: u64,
    pub last_updated: u32, // Avoid unnecessary
fields
}
```

This reduces **storage costs and execution time**.

Gas Optimization in NEAR Smart Contracts

NEAR uses **Wasm execution**, and contracts pay fees based on **storage, computation, and transaction size**.

Reducing Storage Costs with Efficient Data Structures

NEAR provides **UnorderedMap** and **LookupMap**, which are more efficient than **Vectors** for state storage.

Inefficient Approach: Using a Vector for Key-Value Storage

125

```
use near_sdk::collections::Vector;

#[near_bindgen]
#[derive(Default)]
pub struct InefficientContract {
    records: Vector<(String, u64)>,
}
```

A **Vector** is expensive because it **scans through data** to find a specific value.

Optimized Approach: Using LookupMap for O(1) Lookups

```
use near_sdk::collections::LookupMap;

#[near_bindgen]
#[derive(Default)]
pub struct OptimizedContract {
    records: LookupMap<String, u64>,
}
```

This **reduces gas costs by enabling direct lookups**.

Optimizing Contract Execution with Lazy Loading

Instead of **loading all data at once**, use **lazy loading** to retrieve only the necessary data.

```
pub fn get_value(&self, key: String) -> Option<u64>
{
    self.records.get(&key) // Only loads specific
data
}
```

This minimizes **execution costs** and **improves contract performance**.

General Gas Optimization Strategies for Rust Smart Contracts

Regardless of the blockchain, the following strategies improve **gas efficiency and performance**:

Use fixed-size data types instead of dynamically growing structures.

Minimize on-chain computations by performing **heavy processing off-chain**.

Batch transactions to reduce execution overhead.

126

Avoid unnecessary storage writes—only update state when necessary.

Use events instead of state variables for logging information.

For example, instead of storing every user transaction, emit an **event log**:

```
#[ink(event)]
pub struct TransactionRecorded {
    #[ink(topic)]
    sender: AccountId,
    amount: Balance,
}
```

This **reduces storage costs**, as events **do not consume contract state**.

Gas optimization is essential for **ensuring smart contracts remain cost-effective and scalable**.

Ink! contracts should use **Mappings instead of Vectors** and minimize deployment size.

Solana programs should **reduce compute unit consumption** and optimize **account storage**.

NEAR contracts should use **efficient data structures like LookupMap** and implement **lazy loading**.

By carefully designing contracts **to minimize computation and storage costs**, developers can **improve efficiency, lower transaction fees, and enhance contract scalability** across different blockchain platforms.

Using Web3 Libraries to Interact with Contracts

Once a smart contract is deployed, it needs a way to **communicate with users and other applications**. This is where **Web3 libraries** come in. These libraries provide **interfaces that allow frontend applications, scripts, and backend services** to send transactions, read blockchain data, and interact with smart contracts **programmatically**.

Each blockchain ecosystem has **specific Web3 libraries** tailored to its infrastructure. The most widely used Web3 libraries for Rust-based smart contracts include:

Polkadot.js – For interacting with **Ink! contracts** on Polkadot and Substrate-based blockchains.

Solana Web3.js – For connecting to **Solana smart contracts (on-chain programs)**.

NEAR API JS – For communicating with **NEAR smart contracts**.

A Web3 library is a **software toolkit that enables applications to communicate with a blockchain**. It allows developers to:

Read blockchain data (e.g., get account balances, fetch contract states).

Send transactions (e.g., execute smart contract functions).

Listen for blockchain events (e.g., detect changes in contract state).

Instead of **manually constructing blockchain requests**, Web3 libraries handle **low-level blockchain interactions**, making it easier for developers to integrate contracts into **decentralized applications (DApps)**.

Connecting to Ink! Smart Contracts Using Polkadot.js

Ink! smart contracts run on **Substrate-based blockchains** like **Polkadot and Kusama**. The most widely used Web3 library for **Substrate-based contracts** is **Polkadot.js**.

Setting Up Polkadot.js

To interact with an Ink! smart contract, install the `@polkadot/api` package:

```
npm install @polkadot/api
```

Connecting to a Polkadot-Based Blockchain

A Web3 connection to a Substrate blockchain is established using a **WebSocket provider**:

```
const { ApiPromise, WsProvider } =
require('@polkadot/api');
```

```
async function connect() {
    const provider = new
WsProvider('wss://rpc.polkadot.io'); // Connect to
Polkadot network
    const api = await ApiPromise.create({ provider
});

    console.log("Connected to Polkadot
blockchain!");
}

connect();
```

Interacting with an Ink! Smart Contract

To interact with an Ink! contract, you need:

The contract address (where it is deployed).

The contract's ABI (Application Binary Interface), which describes its functions.

Reading a Contract's Stored Value

```
async function readContract(api, contractAddress) {
    const contract = await
api.query.contracts.contractInfoOf(contractAddress)
;

    console.log("Contract info:",
contract.toHuman());
}

readContract(api, '5F3sa2TJ8w...'); // Example
contract address
```

Calling a Contract Function (Writing Data)

To send a transaction and update a contract's state:

```
async function setValue(api, keyring,
contractAddress, newValue) {
    const contract = api.tx.contracts.call(
        contractAddress,
        0, // No attached funds
        1000000000000, // Gas limit
```

129

```
        api.createType('Vec<u8>', newValue)
    );

    const account = keyring.addFromUri('//Alice');
    await contract.signAndSend(account);

    console.log("Value updated successfully!");
}
```

This **updates the stored value** in an Ink! contract using a **Polkadot.js transaction**.

Interacting with Solana Smart Contracts Using Solana Web3.js

Solana's Web3 library, **Solana Web3.js**, allows **frontend and backend applications** to interact with Solana smart contracts (also called on-chain programs).

Installing Solana Web3.js

To interact with Solana programs, install the Solana Web3 library:

```
npm install @solana/web3.js
```

Connecting to the Solana Blockchain

To establish a connection with the Solana network:

```
const { Connection, clusterApiUrl } =
require('@solana/web3.js');

const connection = new
Connection(clusterApiUrl('mainnet-beta'));

console.log("Connected to Solana network");
```

Reading Account Information

A Solana contract stores state data in **accounts**, so reading contract data involves querying an account:

```
const { PublicKey } = require('@solana/web3.js');

async function getAccountData(accountAddress) {
```

```
    const accountInfo = await
connection.getAccountInfo(new
PublicKey(accountAddress));

    console.log("Account Data:", accountInfo.data);
}

getAccountData("5Cq4..."); // Example account
storing contract data
```

Sending Transactions to a Solana Smart Contract

To interact with a deployed Solana contract, **send a transaction** that invokes a program's function:

```
const { Transaction, sendAndConfirmTransaction } =
require('@solana/web3.js');

async function callContract(programId, payer) {
    const transaction = new Transaction().add(
        new TransactionInstruction({
            keys: [{ pubkey: new
PublicKey(programId), isSigner: false, isWritable:
true }],
            programId: new PublicKey(programId),
            data: Buffer.alloc(0) // Example
instruction data
        })
    );

    await sendAndConfirmTransaction(connection,
transaction, [payer]);

    console.log("Transaction sent successfully!");
}
```

This method **sends instructions to execute a smart contract function** on Solana's blockchain.

Interacting with NEAR Smart Contracts Using NearAPI.js

NEAR Protocol provides **NearAPI.js**, a JavaScript SDK for **deploying, calling, and managing NEAR smart contracts**.

Installing NearAPI.js

131

Install the required package:

```
npm install near-api-js
```

Connecting to the NEAR Blockchain

To create a connection, specify the **network and RPC endpoint**:

```
const { connect, keyStores } = require("near-api-js");

async function setupNearConnection() {
    const near = await connect({
        networkId: "testnet",
        keyStore: new keyStores.InMemoryKeyStore(),
        nodeUrl: "https://rpc.testnet.near.org"
    });

    console.log("Connected to NEAR blockchain");
    return near;
}
```

Reading Data from a NEAR Contract

A NEAR smart contract typically **stores data on-chain**, which can be queried:

```
async function getContractValue(contractName) {
    const near = await setupNearConnection();
    const account = await near.account(contractName);

    const contract = new Contract(account, contractName, {
        viewMethods: ["get_value"], // Read-only method
        changeMethods: ["set_value"], // State-changing method
    });

    const value = await contract.get_value();
    console.log("Stored value:", value);
}

getContractValue("mycontract.testnet");
```

Sending Transactions to a NEAR Contract

To update a contract's state, send a transaction:

```
async function updateContractValue(contractName,
newValue) {
    const near = await setupNearConnection();
    const account = await
near.account(contractName);

    const contract = new Contract(account,
contractName, {
        viewMethods: ["get_value"],
        changeMethods: ["set_value"],
    });

    await contract.set_value({ value: newValue });

    console.log("Value updated successfully!");
}

updateContractValue("mycontract.testnet", 42);
```

Web3 libraries make it easy to **connect frontend applications and backend services** to smart contracts.

Polkadot.js enables **Ink! contract interactions on Substrate-based chains**.

Solana Web3.js allows applications to **read from and send transactions to Solana contracts**.

NearAPI.js provides a **simple interface for calling and updating NEAR contracts**.

By using these tools, developers can **seamlessly integrate Rust-based smart contracts into DApps**, enabling **secure and decentralized interactions** between users and blockchain networks.

Chapter 7: Rust-Based Web3 Backends

Web3 backends serve as the **bridge between decentralized applications (DApps) and blockchain networks**. While frontend applications use **Web3.js, Polkadot.js, or NearAPI.js** to interact with smart contracts, backend services handle **data aggregation, authentication, off-chain computations, and API exposure for DApps**.

Rust is a powerful choice for building **Web3 backends** due to its **performance, memory safety, and concurrency support**. Using Rust-based Web3 libraries, developers can build **secure, high-performance backend services** that interact with blockchain networks, query smart contracts, and expose data through **REST or GraphQL APIs**.

Web3 Libraries in Rust (ethers-rs, substrate-api-client)

Rust has become a popular choice for building Web3 applications due to its **performance, memory safety, and concurrency support**. To interact with blockchain networks from a Rust backend, developers use specialized Web3 libraries that provide **tools to query blockchain data, send transactions, and interact with smart contracts**.

Two of the most widely used Rust Web3 libraries are:

`ethers-rs` – A library for interacting with **Ethereum and EVM-compatible blockchains**.

`substrate-api-client` – A library for connecting to **Polkadot, Kusama, and Substrate-based blockchains**.

`ethers-rs`: A Rust Library for Ethereum-Based Blockchains

`ethers-rs` is a **Rust SDK** that allows developers to interact with **Ethereum and other EVM-compatible blockchains** (e.g., Binance Smart Chain, Polygon, Avalanche, Arbitrum). It provides:

RPC connectivity – Connect to Ethereum nodes via **Infura, Alchemy, or self-hosted nodes**.

Contract interactions – Call smart contract functions and send transactions.

Wallet management – Sign and send transactions using Ethereum private keys.

Installing `ethers-rs`

To use `ethers-rs`, add it to your Rust project:

```
[dependencies]
ethers = "2.0"
tokio = { version = "1", features = ["full"] }
dotenv = "0.15"
```

ethers provides Web3 functions for Ethereum.

tokio is an asynchronous runtime required for handling blockchain interactions.

dotenv is useful for managing environment variables such as private keys.

Connecting to an Ethereum Node

To interact with Ethereum, your application needs to connect to an **Ethereum node** using an RPC provider. You can use a service like **Infura, Alchemy, or QuickNode**, or run a local Ethereum node with **Geth or OpenEthereum**.

Here's how to establish a connection:

```
use ethers::prelude::*;
use std::sync::Arc;

#[tokio::main]
async fn main() -> eyre::Result<()> {
    let provider =
Provider::<Http>::try_from("https://mainnet.infura.
io/v3/YOUR_INFURA_KEY")?;
```

```
    let block_number =
provider.get_block_number().await?;
    println!("Latest Ethereum Block: {}",
block_number);

    Ok(())
}
```

This connects to **Ethereum's mainnet**, fetches the latest block number, and prints it.

Reading an Ethereum Account Balance

To retrieve the balance of an Ethereum address:

```
use ethers::types::Address;

#[tokio::main]
async fn main() -> eyre::Result<()> {
    let provider =
Provider::<Http>::try_from("https://mainnet.infura.
io/v3/YOUR_INFURA_KEY")?;

    let wallet_address: Address =
"0x742d35Cc6634C0532925a3b844Bc454e4438f44e".parse(
)?;
    let balance =
provider.get_balance(wallet_address, None).await?;

    println!("ETH Balance: {} ETH",
ethers::utils::format_units(balance, 18)?);

    Ok(())
}
```

This fetches the **ETH balance** of a given wallet address and formats it in **Ether units**.

Interacting with an Ethereum Smart Contract

To interact with a smart contract, you need its **ABI (Application Binary Interface)** and contract address.

Example: Calling a Read-Only Function on an Ethereum Contract

```rust
use ethers::contract::Contract;
use ethers::types::Address;

#[tokio::main]
async fn main() -> eyre::Result<()> {
    let provider =
Provider::<Http>::try_from("https://mainnet.infura.
io/v3/YOUR_INFURA_KEY")?;

    let contract_address: Address =
"0x123456789abcdef...".parse()?;
    let abi = include_bytes!("contract_abi.json");
// Load ABI from a JSON file

    let contract = Contract::from_json(provider,
contract_address, abi)?;

    let value: U256 = contract.method("getValue",
())?.call().await?;
    println!("Contract value: {}", value);

    Ok(())
}
```

This reads a **public state variable** from an Ethereum smart contract.

Sending a Transaction to a Smart Contract

To send a **state-changing transaction**, a wallet **must sign and send it**:

```rust
use ethers::signers::Wallet;
use ethers::types::TransactionRequest;

#[tokio::main]
async fn main() -> eyre::Result<()> {
    let provider =
Provider::<Http>::try_from("https://mainnet.infura.
io/v3/YOUR_INFURA_KEY")?;
    let wallet =
"YOUR_PRIVATE_KEY".parse::<Wallet>()?;
    let client = SignerMiddleware::new(provider,
wallet);

    let tx = TransactionRequest::new()
```

```
        .to("0x123456789abcdef...")
        .value(ethers::utils::parse_ether("0.1")?);

    let pending_tx = client.send_transaction(tx,
None).await?;
    println!("Transaction sent: {:?}",
pending_tx.tx_hash());

    Ok(())
}
```

This sends **0.1 ETH** to another address.

`substrate-api-client`: A Rust Library for Polkadot and Substrate-Based Blockchains

`substrate-api-client` is a **Rust SDK** that allows developers to interact with **Polkadot, Kusama, and Substrate-based blockchains**. It provides:

RPC connectivity – Connect to any **Substrate-based blockchain**.

State querying – Read balances, contract storage, and network status.

Transaction execution – Send signed transactions to interact with smart contracts or transfer tokens.

Installing `substrate-api-client`

To add `substrate-api-client` to a Rust project:

```
[dependencies]
substrate-api-client = "0.11"
tokio = { version = "1", features = ["full"] }
```

Connecting to a Polkadot Node

To query the **latest block** from Polkadot's blockchain:

```
use substrate_api_client::{Api, WsRpcClient};

fn main() {
    let client =
WsRpcClient::new("wss://rpc.polkadot.io");
    let api = Api::new(client).unwrap();
```

```
    let block_hash =
api.get_finalized_head().unwrap();
    println!("Latest Polkadot Block Hash: {:?}",
block_hash);
}
```

This fetches the **most recent finalized block** from the Polkadot blockchain.

Querying an Account's Balance on Polkadot

To get a wallet's **DOT balance**:

```
fn get_balance(api: &Api<WsRpcClient>, account_id:
&str) {
    let balance =
api.get_storage_value::<u128>("Balances",
"FreeBalance", account_id);
    println!("Balance: {:?}", balance);
}
```

Sending a Transaction on Polkadot

To send **tokens from one account to another**, a transaction must be signed:

```
use substrate_api_client::AccountKeyring;

fn transfer(api: &mut Api<WsRpcClient>) {
    let sender = AccountKeyring::Alice.pair();
    let recipient =
AccountKeyring::Bob.to_account_id();

    let tx =
api.balance_transfer(recipient.clone(),
10_000_000_000);
    let result = api.send_extrinsic(tx, sender);

    println!("Transaction result: {:?}", result);
}
```

This **transfers DOT tokens** from Alice to Bob.

Rust provides powerful Web3 libraries for interacting with blockchain networks:

`ethers-rs` is the **go-to library for Ethereum** and all **EVM-compatible blockchains**.

`substrate-api-client` enables **direct interactions with Polkadot, Kusama, and Substrate-based chains**.

By leveraging these libraries, developers can **build fast, secure, and efficient Web3 backends** that interact with smart contracts and blockchain networks.

Connecting to Blockchain Networks with Rust

A blockchain network is a decentralized system where transactions and smart contract interactions are recorded and verified by a distributed set of nodes. To interact with these networks, applications need a **connection layer** that allows them to **query blockchain data, send transactions, and subscribe to events**.

Rust provides powerful Web3 libraries such as `ethers-rs` for Ethereum-based blockchains and `substrate-api-client` for Polkadot and Substrate-based blockchains. These libraries enable backend services and decentralized applications (DApps) to establish secure and efficient blockchain connections.

To interact with a blockchain, an application must connect to a **full node** or a **remote procedure call (RPC) provider**.

Types of Blockchain Nodes

Full Nodes – Store the entire blockchain history and validate transactions independently.

Light Nodes – Store only necessary data, relying on full nodes for transaction validation.

RPC Nodes – Provide APIs for querying blockchain data and submitting transactions.

A **full node** is required for maximum security, but most applications use **RPC providers** such as **Infura, Alchemy, or public RPC endpoints** to avoid the overhead of maintaining their own nodes.

Connecting to Ethereum Using `ethers-rs`

Ethereum is an **EVM-compatible** blockchain where smart contracts execute **state-changing operations** through transactions. To interact with Ethereum, a Rust application must connect to an Ethereum **RPC endpoint** using `ethers-rs`.

Installing `ethers-rs`

To integrate `ethers-rs` into a Rust project, add the following dependencies to `Cargo.toml`:

```
[dependencies]
ethers = "2.0"
tokio = { version = "1", features = ["full"] }
dotenv = "0.15"
```

Connecting to an Ethereum RPC Provider

An Ethereum RPC provider allows applications to send transactions and query data from the blockchain. Infura, Alchemy, and QuickNode provide **hosted Ethereum RPC endpoints**, while Geth and OpenEthereum allow developers to run their own nodes.

```
use ethers::prelude::*;
use std::sync::Arc;

#[tokio::main]
async fn main() -> eyre::Result<()> {
    let provider =
Provider::<Http>::try_from("https://mainnet.infura.
io/v3/YOUR_INFURA_KEY")?;

    let block_number =
provider.get_block_number().await?;
    println!("Latest Ethereum Block: {}",
block_number);

    Ok(())
}
```

This connects to Ethereum's **mainnet** using **Infura** and retrieves the latest block number.

Querying Ethereum Account Balances

To fetch an Ethereum account's **ETH balance**, use the following function:

```
use ethers::types::Address;

#[tokio::main]
async fn main() -> eyre::Result<()> {
    let provider =
Provider::<Http>::try_from("https://mainnet.infura.
io/v3/YOUR_INFURA_KEY")?;

    let address: Address =
"0x742d35Cc6634C0532925a3b844Bc454e4438f44e".parse(
)?;
    let balance = provider.get_balance(address,
None).await?;

    println!("Balance: {} ETH",
ethers::utils::format_units(balance, 18)?);

    Ok(())
}
```

This fetches the ETH balance of the given wallet and formats it correctly in **Ether units**.

Connecting to Polkadot and Substrate-Based Blockchains Using `substrate-api-client`

Polkadot and Kusama are **Substrate-based blockchains** that allow developers to build custom blockchains with interoperable smart contracts. Rust applications can connect to these blockchains using `substrate-api-client`.

Installing `substrate-api-client`

Add the `substrate-api-client` dependency to `Cargo.toml`:

```
[dependencies]
substrate-api-client = "0.11"
tokio = { version = "1", features = ["full"] }
```

Connecting to a Polkadot RPC Node

A Rust application can connect to a Polkadot node via **WebSocket RPC**. Public endpoints include:

Polkadot Mainnet: `wss://rpc.polkadot.io`

Kusama Mainnet: `wss://kusama-rpc.polkadot.io`

Substrate Development Node: `ws://127.0.0.1:9944`

```
use substrate_api_client::{Api, WsRpcClient};

fn main() {
    let client =
WsRpcClient::new("wss://rpc.polkadot.io");
    let api = Api::new(client).unwrap();

    let block_hash =
api.get_finalized_head().unwrap();
    println!("Latest Polkadot Block Hash: {:?}",
block_hash);
}
```

This fetches the **most recent finalized block** from the Polkadot network.

Querying an Account's DOT Balance

To retrieve an account's balance on Polkadot:

```
fn get_balance(api: &Api<WsRpcClient>, account_id:
&str) {
    let balance =
api.get_storage_value::<u128>("Balances",
"FreeBalance", account_id);
    println!("Balance: {:?}", balance);
}
```

This queries the on-chain storage to fetch the **current balance of a Polkadot account**.

Running a Local Blockchain Node for Testing

For local development, running a **private blockchain node** allows developers to test transactions and contract interactions without spending real tokens.

Running a Local Ethereum Node with Geth

Geth is an **Ethereum client** that allows developers to run a full Ethereum node:

```
geth --dev --http --http.api eth,net,web3 --
http.port 8545
```

This starts a **local Ethereum testnet** at `http://127.0.0.1:8545`. Applications can connect to it instead of using an external RPC provider.

Running a Local Polkadot Node with Substrate

To test Substrate-based applications locally, use a **Substrate development node**:

```
substrate --dev
```

This starts a **local Substrate blockchain** that can be used for smart contract testing.

Handling Connection Errors and Network Failures

A blockchain network may experience **RPC failures, high latency, or node downtime**. A Rust application should **gracefully handle these issues** by:

Retrying failed connections with exponential backoff.

Using multiple RPC providers as failovers.

Handling connection timeouts to avoid blocking execution.

Example: Retrying an Ethereum Connection

```rust
use ethers::prelude::*;
use std::time::Duration;
use tokio::time::sleep;

#[tokio::main]
async fn main() -> eyre::Result<()> {
    let provider = loop {
        match
Provider::<Http>::try_from("https://mainnet.infura.
io/v3/YOUR_INFURA_KEY") {
            Ok(p) => break p,
```

```
            Err(_) => {
                println!("Connection failed.
Retrying...");

sleep(Duration::from_secs(5)).await;
            }
        }
    };

    let block_number =
provider.get_block_number().await?;
    println!("Latest Ethereum Block: {}",
block_number);

    Ok(())
}
```

This ensures the application **keeps trying to reconnect** if the blockchain node is temporarily unavailable.

Connecting a Rust application to a blockchain network requires:

Choosing the right Web3 library (`ethers-rs` for Ethereum, `substrate-api-client` for Polkadot).

Using a reliable RPC provider (Infura, Alchemy, or a self-hosted node).

Handling network failures gracefully to maintain uptime.

Using local blockchain nodes for testing and development.

By implementing these techniques, developers can build **efficient, scalable, and resilient Web3 backends** that interact with decentralized networks securely and reliably.

Building REST and GraphQL APIs for DApps

Decentralized applications (DApps) rely on **smart contracts** to execute transactions on a blockchain, but direct interaction with blockchain nodes is **inefficient and impractical** for frontend applications. Instead, a **Web3 backend** acts as an intermediary, providing an optimized interface for querying blockchain data, sending transactions, and managing off-chain computations.

The two most commonly used API architectures for Web3 backends are **REST (Representational State Transfer)** and **GraphQL (Graph Query Language)**. These APIs allow DApps to efficiently retrieve **account balances, transaction history, contract states, and other blockchain data** while ensuring scalability and security.

Why DApps Need REST and GraphQL APIs

Most blockchains are **not optimized for direct frontend queries**. Unlike traditional databases, blockchains:

Do **not support SQL-like queries** for filtering and aggregation.

Require applications to **connect to full nodes** to fetch data.

Charge **gas fees for on-chain computations**, making frequent queries costly.

A **REST or GraphQL API** simplifies blockchain access by:

Caching frequently requested data to reduce blockchain queries.

Preprocessing and filtering data off-chain to reduce gas costs.

Providing structured endpoints that DApps can call without requiring direct blockchain interactions.

Building a REST API for DApps Using Actix-Web

Installing Actix-Web

Actix-Web is a **high-performance web framework for Rust**, widely used for building REST APIs. Add it to your project:

```
[dependencies]
actix-web = "4"
ethers = "2.0"
substrate-api-client = "0.11"
tokio = { version = "1", features = ["full"] }
serde = { version = "1", features = ["derive"] }
```

Setting Up a Basic REST API

The following Rust program creates an **Actix-Web REST API** that listens for HTTP requests and responds with blockchain data.

```rust
use actix_web::{web, App, HttpServer, Responder};
use ethers::prelude::*;
use std::sync::Arc;

#[tokio::main]
async fn main() -> std::io::Result<()> {
    HttpServer::new(|| {
        App::new()
            .route("/",
web::get().to(health_check))
            .route("/latest-block",
web::get().to(get_latest_block))
    })
    .bind("127.0.0.1:8080")?
    .run()
    .await
}

async fn health_check() -> impl Responder {
    "API is running!"
}

async fn get_latest_block() -> impl Responder {
    let provider =
Provider::<Http>::try_from("https://mainnet.infura.
io/v3/YOUR_INFURA_KEY").unwrap();
    let block_number =
provider.get_block_number().await.unwrap();

    format!("Latest Ethereum Block: {}",
block_number)
}
```

Running the API Server

To start the API, run:

147

```
cargo run
```

Now, sending a GET request to `http://127.0.0.1:8080/latest-block` will return:

```
{

    "block_number": 15234567

}
```

Adding an Endpoint to Fetch Account Balances

A REST API should allow users to query their **Ethereum or Polkadot balances**. The following example adds an endpoint to fetch an Ethereum account's ETH balance:

```rust
use ethers::types::Address;
use serde::Serialize;

#[derive(Serialize)]
struct BalanceResponse {
    balance: String,
}

async fn get_balance(path: web::Path<String>) ->
impl Responder {
    let provider =
Provider::<Http>::try_from("https://mainnet.infura.
io/v3/YOUR_INFURA_KEY").unwrap();

    let address: Address =
path.into_inner().parse().unwrap();
    let balance = provider.get_balance(address,
None).await.unwrap();
    let formatted_balance =
ethers::utils::format_units(balance, 18).unwrap();

    web::Json(BalanceResponse { balance:
formatted_balance })
}
```

Now, sending a GET request to
```
/balance/0x742d35Cc6634C0532925a3b844Bc454e4438f44e
```
returns:
```
{
    "balance": "123.45"
}
```

Building a GraphQL API for DApps Using Juniper

GraphQL provides **flexibility** that REST APIs lack. Instead of returning **predefined endpoints**, GraphQL allows clients to request **only the data they need**, reducing response size and improving efficiency.

For example, a REST request might return **all transaction details**, even if the client only needs the sender's address. With GraphQL, the client can specify **which fields to retrieve**, reducing unnecessary data transfer.

Installing Juniper (GraphQL for Rust)

Juniper is a **GraphQL framework for Rust** that integrates well with Actix-Web. Install it:

```
[dependencies]
juniper = "0.15"
actix-web = "4"
tokio = { version = "1", features = ["full"] }
ethers = "2.0"
serde = { version = "1", features = ["derive"] }
```

Setting Up a GraphQL Schema

A **GraphQL schema** defines the structure of API queries. The following example creates a **GraphQL API that fetches Ethereum account balances**.

```
use juniper::{graphql_object, EmptyMutation,
EmptySubscription, RootNode};
use ethers::prelude::*;
use std::sync::Arc;

struct Query;
```

149

```rust
#[graphql_object]
impl Query {
    async fn balance(address: String) -> String {
        let provider =
Provider::<Http>::try_from("https://mainnet.infura.
io/v3/YOUR_INFURA_KEY").unwrap();
        let addr =
address.parse::<Address>().unwrap();
        let balance = provider.get_balance(addr,
None).await.unwrap();

        ethers::utils::format_units(balance,
18).unwrap()
    }
}

type Schema = RootNode<'static, Query,
EmptyMutation<()>, EmptySubscription<()>>;

fn schema() -> Schema {
    Schema::new(Query, EmptyMutation::new(),
EmptySubscription::new())
}
```

Exposing GraphQL Queries Using Actix-Web

Now, integrate the GraphQL schema with Actix-Web to **expose GraphQL queries over HTTP**.

```rust
use actix_web::{web, App, HttpServer};
use juniper_actix::graphql_handler;

#[actix_web::main]
async fn main() -> std::io::Result<()> {
    let schema = web::Data::new(schema());

    HttpServer::new(move || {
        App::new()
            .app_data(schema.clone())
            .route("/graphql",
web::post().to(graphql_handler))
    })
```

```
    .bind("127.0.0.1:8080")?
    .run()
    .await
}
```

Querying the GraphQL API

To fetch an Ethereum account balance using GraphQL, send the following query:

```
{
    balance(address:
"0x742d35Cc6634C0532925a3b844Bc454e4438f44e")
}
Response:
{
    "data": {
        "balance": "123.45"
    }
}
```

This API **efficiently returns only the requested data**, unlike REST, which returns **predefined structures**.

Deploying the API

Once the API is built, deploy it using:

Docker for containerization.

AWS Lambda or Google Cloud Functions for serverless hosting.

Heroku, DigitalOcean, or Kubernetes for traditional hosting.

For Docker deployment, create a **Dockerfile**:

```
FROM rust:latest
WORKDIR /app
COPY . .
RUN cargo build --release
CMD ["./target/release/my_api"]
```

Then build and run the container:

```
docker build -t my_api .
docker run -p 8080:8080 my_api
```

151

A well-structured **REST or GraphQL API** simplifies how DApps interact with blockchains by:

Reducing direct node queries through caching and preprocessing.

Providing structured data access for account balances, transactions, and contract state.

Enhancing performance by handling **off-chain computations**.

Using **Actix-Web for REST and Juniper for GraphQL**, Rust developers can build **scalable, efficient, and secure Web3 backends** for decentralized applications.

Chapter 8: Frontend Integration for Rust-Based DApps

A decentralized application (DApp) consists of two major components:

A blockchain backend that handles smart contract interactions, transaction processing, and data storage.

A frontend interface that allows users to interact with the blockchain through a web or mobile application.

When building a **Rust-based backend**, integrating it with a frontend built using **JavaScript, TypeScript, or WebAssembly (Wasm)** is essential for **seamless user experience and blockchain connectivity**.

Connecting Rust Backends to JavaScript/TypeScript

Modern web applications often require a **fast, reliable, and secure backend** to process requests, handle data, and communicate with external systems. Rust has emerged as a powerful backend language due to its **performance, memory safety, and concurrency model**. Meanwhile, JavaScript and TypeScript dominate frontend development, making the ability to integrate Rust backends with JavaScript/TypeScript frontends an essential skill.

A web backend needs to **handle requests, process data, and return responses**. Rust has several frameworks for this purpose, with **Actix-Web** being one of the most popular due to its **speed, scalability, and async support**.

Setting Up the Rust Backend

Start by creating a new Rust project for the backend:

```
cargo new rust_backend
cd rust_backend
```

Modify `Cargo.toml` to include necessary dependencies:

```
[dependencies]
```

```
actix-web = "4"
serde = { version = "1.0", features = ["derive"] }
serde_json = "1.0"
tokio = { version = "1", features = ["full"] }
```

Implementing a REST API in Rust

The following Rust server **exposes a REST API** that provides an endpoint to fetch a message:

```
use actix_web::{get, web, App, HttpServer,
Responder};
use serde::Serialize;

#[derive(Serialize)]
struct MessageResponse {
    message: String,
}

#[get("/api/message")]
async fn get_message() -> impl Responder {
    let response = MessageResponse {
        message: "Hello from Rust
backend!".to_string(),
    };

    web::Json(response)
}

#[actix_web::main]
async fn main() -> std::io::Result<()> {
    HttpServer::new(||
App::new().service(get_message))
        .bind("127.0.0.1:8080")?
        .run()
        .await
}
```

Starting the Rust Server

Run the following command to start the server:

```
cargo run
Once the server is running, accessing
http://127.0.0.1:8080/api/message should return:
```

154

```
{
    "message": "Hello from Rust backend!"
}
```

Connecting the JavaScript/TypeScript Frontend

Now that the Rust backend is running, the frontend can interact with it using **JavaScript or TypeScript**.

Setting Up a React Frontend

For simplicity, let's use **React.js** to build the frontend. If you prefer **TypeScript**, add `--template typescript`.

```
npx create-react-app js_frontend
cd js_frontend
```

Fetching Data from the Rust Backend

Modify the `App.js` file in React to fetch and display data from the Rust backend:

```
import React, { useEffect, useState } from "react";

function App() {
    const [message, setMessage] = useState("");

    useEffect(() => {
        fetch("http://127.0.0.1:8080/api/message")
            .then(response => response.json())
            .then(data => setMessage(data.message))
            .catch(error => console.error("Error
fetching data:", error));
    }, []);

    return (
        <div>
            <h1>{message}</h1>
        </div>
    );
}

export default App;
```

Running the React Application

Start the React development server:

npm start

Now, when you open the browser at `http://localhost:3000/`, you should see **"Hello from Rust backend!"** displayed on the screen.

Using WebSockets for Real-Time Communication

While REST APIs are useful for **request-response communication**, real-time applications (such as chat apps or live notifications) require **WebSockets**.

Implementing WebSockets in Rust

Modify `Cargo.toml` to include the Warp framework, which supports WebSockets:

```
[dependencies]
warp = "0.3"
tokio = { version = "1", features = ["full"] }
```

Create a WebSocket server that sends messages every few seconds:

```
use warp::Filter;
use tokio::sync::broadcast;
use tokio::time::{self, Duration};

#[tokio::main]
async fn main() {
    let (tx, _) = broadcast::channel::<String>(10);
    let tx_clone = tx.clone();

    tokio::spawn(async move {
        let mut interval =
time::interval(Duration::from_secs(3));
        loop {
            interval.tick().await;
            let _ = tx_clone.send("New event from
Rust backend!".to_string());
        }
    });

    let websocket_route = warp::path("ws")
```

```rust
        .and(warp::ws())
        .map(move |ws: warp::ws::Ws| {
            let tx = tx.clone();
            ws.on_upgrade(move |socket| async move
{
                let mut rx = tx.subscribe();
                while let Ok(message) =
rx.recv().await {
                    let _ =
socket.send(warp::ws::Message::text(message)).await
;
                }
            })
        });

    warp::serve(websocket_route).run(([127, 0, 0,
1], 3030)).await;
}
```

Connecting JavaScript to the WebSocket Server

Modify the `App.js` file to listen for WebSocket messages:

```javascript
import React, { useEffect, useState } from "react";

function App() {
    const [message, setMessage] = useState("");

    useEffect(() => {
        const ws = new
WebSocket("ws://127.0.0.1:3030/ws");
        ws.onmessage = (event) => {
            setMessage(event.data);
        };

        return () => ws.close();
    }, []);

    return (
        <div>
            <h1>{message}</h1>
        </div>
```

```
    );
}
```

```
export default App;
```

Now, every **three seconds**, the WebSocket server will send an event, and the frontend will display it in real-time.

Using WebAssembly (Wasm) to Run Rust in the Browser

WebAssembly (Wasm) allows Rust code to run directly in the browser, improving performance for **cryptographic computations, blockchain interactions, and data processing**.

Setting Up Rust for WebAssembly

Install the WebAssembly toolchain:

```
rustup target add wasm32-unknown-unknown
cargo install wasm-pack
```

Creating a Rust Library for WebAssembly

Modify Cargo.toml to include:

```
[dependencies]
wasm-bindgen = "0.2"
```

Create a function in Rust that returns a message:

```
use wasm_bindgen::prelude::*;

#[wasm_bindgen]
pub fn get_message() -> String {
    "Hello from Rust and WebAssembly!".to_string()
}
```

Compile the Rust code to WebAssembly:

```
wasm-pack build --target web
```

Integrating WebAssembly into JavaScript

In your React project, import and call the Rust function:

```
import init, { get_message } from
"./pkg/rust_wasm.js";

async function runWasm() {
```

```
    await init();
    console.log(get_message());
}

runWasm();
```

Now, the frontend **runs Rust code in the browser**, leveraging WebAssembly for performance-critical tasks.

Integrating a **Rust backend** with a **JavaScript/TypeScript frontend** creates a **fast, secure, and efficient web application**.

REST APIs using Actix-Web provide structured data access.

WebSockets enable real-time updates.

WebAssembly (Wasm) allows high-performance Rust execution in the browser.

By combining these technologies, developers can build **scalable, decentralized, and performant** applications that harness the power of Rust while maintaining the flexibility of JavaScript-based frontends.

Using WebAssembly (Wasm) with Rust

WebAssembly (Wasm) is a **binary instruction format** that allows code written in languages like Rust to run **efficiently and securely in the browser**. It is designed for high performance, enabling developers to execute **low-level operations, cryptographic functions, and computationally expensive tasks** directly in a web environment.

Rust is particularly well-suited for WebAssembly because it **compiles to Wasm natively, ensures memory safety without garbage collection, and optimizes performance**. This makes Rust an excellent choice for building applications that require **speed, security, and portability** while leveraging modern web technologies.

Why Use WebAssembly with Rust?

Performance and Efficiency

159

JavaScript, despite its improvements, **is not optimized for CPU-intensive tasks** like cryptographic hashing, physics simulations, or real-time image processing. WebAssembly allows these tasks to be handled **at near-native speeds**.

Memory Safety

Unlike C or C++, Rust guarantees **memory safety without garbage collection**. This means that Rust-Wasm modules can run **efficiently** without the performance overhead of JavaScript's automatic memory management.

Interoperability with JavaScript

WebAssembly doesn't replace JavaScript but works **alongside it**, enabling JavaScript to handle UI interactions while Wasm processes complex computations.

Setting Up Rust for WebAssembly Development

To get started with WebAssembly in Rust, you need to install the **Wasm toolchain** and set up a Rust project that compiles to WebAssembly.

Step 1: Install Rust and WebAssembly Target

Ensure Rust is installed:

```
curl --proto '=https' --tlsv1.2 -sSf
https://sh.rustup.rs | sh
```

Then, add WebAssembly as a compilation target:

```
rustup target add wasm32-unknown-unknown
```

This tells Rust to compile programs to **WebAssembly format** instead of native machine code.

Step 2: Install `wasm-pack`

`wasm-pack` simplifies the process of **compiling Rust code to WebAssembly and generating JavaScript bindings**. Install it with:

```
cargo install wasm-pack
```

Writing a Rust WebAssembly Module

Let's write a simple Rust function that **adds two numbers** and compile it to WebAssembly.

Step 1: Create a New Rust Library

Navigate to your project directory and create a new Rust library:

```
cargo new --lib rust_wasm_demo
cd rust_wasm_demo
```

Modify the `Cargo.toml` file to include:

```
[dependencies]
wasm-bindgen = "0.2"
```

The `wasm-bindgen` crate allows Rust to **interact with JavaScript** by generating bindings.

Step 2: Write the Rust Function

Modify `src/lib.rs` to define a simple function that adds two numbers:

```
use wasm_bindgen::prelude::*;

// Expose the function to JavaScript
#[wasm_bindgen]
pub fn add_numbers(a: i32, b: i32) -> i32 {
    a + b
}
```

This function takes two integers, adds them, and returns the result.

Compiling Rust to WebAssembly

Compile the Rust library into WebAssembly using:

```
wasm-pack build --target web
```

This command generates a `pkg/` directory containing:

The `.wasm` binary file.

JavaScript bindings (`.js`) that allow JavaScript to call Rust functions.

Integrating Rust WebAssembly with JavaScript

161

Once compiled, you can import the Wasm module into a JavaScript project.

Step 1: Set Up a Simple HTML Page

Create an `index.html` file:

```html
<!DOCTYPE html>
<html lang="en">
<head>
    <meta charset="UTF-8">
    <title>Rust and WebAssembly</title>
</head>
<body>
    <h1>Wasm Example</h1>
    <p>Result: <span id="result"></span></p>

    <script type="module">
        import init, { add_numbers } from
"./pkg/rust_wasm_demo.js";

        async function runWasm() {
            await init();
            const result = add_numbers(5, 10);

document.getElementById("result").textContent =
result;
        }

        runWasm();
    </script>
</body>
</html>
```

This **loads the WebAssembly module**, calls the Rust function, and updates the webpage with the result.

Step 2: Start a Local Server

For security reasons, WebAssembly must be loaded from a server. You can use Python's built-in HTTP server:

python3 -m http.server 8080

Open `http://localhost:8080` in a browser, and it should display:

162

Real-World Applications of Rust and WebAssembly

Cryptographic Operations

Rust's WebAssembly modules are ideal for handling **digital signatures, encryption, and hashing** directly in the browser.

Example:
A Rust function that generates a **SHA-256 hash** from a given input:

```
use wasm_bindgen::prelude::*;
use sha2::{Sha256, Digest};

#[wasm_bindgen]
pub fn sha256_hash(input: &str) -> String {
    let mut hasher = Sha256::new();
    hasher.update(input);
    format!("{:x}", hasher.finalize())
}
```

JavaScript can call this function to hash a user's password **without exposing it to the server**.

Blockchain and Smart Contracts

WebAssembly allows DApps to process transactions **locally in the browser**, reducing network calls.

For example, a **Rust WebAssembly module** can **validate Ethereum addresses**:

```
use wasm_bindgen::prelude::*;
use regex::Regex;

#[wasm_bindgen]
pub fn is_valid_ethereum_address(address: &str) ->
bool {
    let re = Regex::new(r"^0x[a-fA-F0-
9]{40}$").unwrap();
    re.is_match(address)
}
```

This function enables a DApp to validate user inputs **instantly**, improving security and UX.

Machine Learning in the Browser

With WebAssembly, Rust can run **machine learning inference models** directly in a web application without relying on backend servers.

For example, using **TensorFlow Lite** in Rust-Wasm can speed up **real-time image recognition** in a browser-based application.

Best Practices for Rust and WebAssembly

Optimize for Size: Use `wasm-opt` to reduce Wasm file sizes.

```
wasm-opt -O3 pkg/rust_wasm_demo_bg.wasm -o
pkg/rust_wasm_demo_bg_opt.wasm
```

Reduce Unnecessary Memory Allocation: Avoid passing large arrays or objects between Rust and JavaScript frequently.

Use Streaming Compilation: Load Wasm asynchronously to **prevent blocking the main thread**.

Leverage Rust's `wee_alloc` for Smaller Binaries:

```
[dependencies]
wee_alloc = { version = "0.4", optional = true }
```

Using Rust with WebAssembly enables **high-performance, memory-safe, and secure execution** of code in the browser. By compiling Rust to Wasm, developers can:

Run Rust functions directly in JavaScript applications.

Optimize performance for cryptography, blockchain processing, and machine learning.

Enhance security and efficiency in DApps by processing sensitive data **locally in the browser**.

By integrating **Rust, WebAssembly, and JavaScript**, developers can **build modern, fast, and scalable web applications** while leveraging Rust's performance and safety guarantees.

Creating Decentralized Frontends

A **decentralized frontend** is a user interface that interacts directly with blockchain networks, smart contracts, and peer-to-peer storage systems without relying on centralized servers. Unlike traditional web applications, where a backend processes requests and serves data, decentralized applications (**DApps**) use blockchain infrastructure and decentralized file storage to operate without a single point of failure.

To build an effective decentralized frontend, developers need to integrate **blockchain interactions, decentralized storage, wallet authentication, and smart contract calls** into the user interface. This requires working with **Web3 libraries, smart contract platforms, and decentralized hosting solutions** to ensure security, scalability, and censorship resistance.

A **traditional frontend** relies on centralized APIs and databases, meaning users must trust a **single entity** to store and process data. In contrast, a **decentralized frontend** connects to:

Smart contracts: Programs deployed on the blockchain that execute transactions automatically.

Wallet providers: Users sign transactions using their own wallets (e.g., MetaMask, Phantom, Polkadot.js).

Decentralized storage: Instead of centralized servers, files are stored on **IPFS, Arweave, or Filecoin**.

A decentralized frontend does not rely on a backend for authentication, as users interact directly with the blockchain. This enhances privacy and security while reducing risks associated with **server failures or data breaches**.

Setting Up a Decentralized React Frontend

165

A modern decentralized frontend is typically built with **React** or **Vue.js**, which provides a dynamic and interactive interface. Let's create a **React DApp** that interacts with a **Rust-based smart contract** deployed on an **EVM-compatible blockchain** (Ethereum, Polygon, Arbitrum).

Step 1: Set Up a React Frontend

To create a new React application, run:

```
npx create-react-app decentralized-frontend
cd decentralized-frontend
```

If using **TypeScript**, append `--template typescript`:

```
npx create-react-app decentralized-frontend --template typescript
```

Step 2: Install Web3 Dependencies

To connect the frontend to a blockchain, install **ethers.js**:

```
npm install ethers
```

For interacting with **Polkadot-based blockchains**, install **@polkadot/api**:

```
npm install @polkadot/api
```

Step 3: Connect the Frontend to a Blockchain Wallet

Users interact with the blockchain through a **wallet provider** like **MetaMask**. The frontend needs to detect the wallet and request permission to connect.

Modify `App.js` (or `App.tsx` for TypeScript) to include wallet detection:

```
import React, { useState, useEffect } from "react";
import { ethers } from "ethers";

function App() {
    const [account, setAccount] = useState(null);

    async function connectWallet() {
        if (window.ethereum) {
            const provider = new ethers.providers.Web3Provider(window.ethereum);
            await window.ethereum.request({ method: "eth_requestAccounts" });
            const signer = provider.getSigner();
```

```
            const userAddress = await
signer.getAddress();
            setAccount(userAddress);
        } else {
            alert("No Ethereum wallet found. Please
install MetaMask.");
        }
    }

    return (
        <div>
            <h1>Decentralized Frontend</h1>
            {account ? <p>Connected: {account}</p>
: <button onClick={connectWallet}>Connect
Wallet</button>}
        </div>
    );
}

export default App;
```

When the user clicks "Connect Wallet," the application requests access to their **Ethereum wallet**, allowing them to sign transactions.

Integrating a Rust Smart Contract

Compiling a Rust Smart Contract to WebAssembly

Rust smart contracts compiled to **WebAssembly (Wasm)** can be deployed on **Substrate-based blockchains** (Polkadot, Kusama).

Install the **Rust WebAssembly toolchain**:

```
rustup target add wasm32-unknown-unknown
```

Then, create a new Rust smart contract using **Ink!**:

```
cargo contract new rust_smart_contract
cd rust_smart_contract
```

Modify lib.rs to define a contract that **stores and retrieves a value**:

```
#![cfg_attr(not(feature = "std"), no_std)]

use ink_lang as ink;
```

```
#[ink::contract]
mod rust_contract {
    #[ink(storage)]
    pub struct RustContract {
        value: u32,
    }

    impl RustContract {
        #[ink(constructor)]
        pub fn new(init_value: u32) -> Self {
            Self { value: init_value }
        }

        #[ink(message)]
        pub fn set_value(&mut self, new_value: u32)
{

            self.value = new_value;
        }

        #[ink(message)]
        pub fn get_value(&self) -> u32 {
            self.value
        }
    }
}
```

Compile the contract to Wasm:

cargo contract build

Deploy the `.wasm` contract file on **Polkadot's contracts pallet** using **Polkadot.js Apps**.

Interacting with the Smart Contract from the Frontend

Modify App.js to allow users to **call smart contract functions**:

```
import React, { useEffect, useState } from "react";
import { ApiPromise, WsProvider } from
"@polkadot/api";

function App() {
    const [contractValue, setContractValue] =
useState(null);
```

```
    async function fetchContractValue() {
        const provider = new
WsProvider("wss://rpc.polkadot.io");
        const api = await ApiPromise.create({
provider });
        const contractAddress = "5F3sa2TJ8w..."; //
Replace with deployed contract address
        const storage = await
api.query.contracts.contractInfoOf(contractAddress)
;
        setContractValue(storage.toHuman());
    }

    useEffect(() => {
        fetchContractValue();
    }, []);

    return (
        <div>
            <h1>Decentralized Frontend</h1>
            <p>Stored Contract Value:
{contractValue}</p>
        </div>
    );
}

export default App;
```

This fetches **on-chain data** and updates the UI accordingly.

Storing Data in a Decentralized Manner

Frontend files and metadata should not be stored on centralized servers.
Instead, use **IPFS (InterPlanetary File System)** for decentralized hosting.

Uploading Frontend Files to IPFS

Install `ipfs-http-client`:

```
npm install ipfs-http-client
```
Modify `App.js` to upload a file to IPFS:

```
import { create } from "ipfs-http-client";
```

```
const ipfs = create({ host: "ipfs.infura.io", port:
5001, protocol: "https" });

async function uploadToIPFS(file) {
    const added = await ipfs.add(file);
    console.log("File uploaded to IPFS:",
added.path);
}
```

This ensures **frontend assets are immutable and accessible globally**, even if a traditional web server is down.

Deploying the Decentralized Frontend

To make the frontend **fully decentralized**, deploy it on **IPFS**:

```
npm install -g fleek-cli
fleek init
fleek deploy
```

Other hosting solutions include **Arweave, Skynet, and Filecoin**.

A **decentralized frontend** eliminates the need for centralized servers by integrating **Web3 wallets, smart contracts, and decentralized storage**. By using **Rust for smart contracts and JavaScript/TypeScript for the UI**, developers can build **fast, secure, and censorship-resistant applications** that are controlled entirely by users.

By combining **React, Rust, IPFS, and blockchain technology**, a decentralized frontend provides a **trustless, self-sustaining ecosystem** that **empowers users** rather than central authorities.

Chapter 9: Decentralized Storage and Off-Chain Computation

Blockchain applications are designed to be **transparent, tamper-proof, and decentralized**. However, storing large amounts of data and performing complex computations **directly on-chain** can be inefficient and expensive.

Smart contracts have strict limitations on **storage and processing power**, making it impractical to store large files or run computationally heavy operations directly on the blockchain. Instead, developers use **decentralized storage solutions** like **IPFS and Arweave** for data storage, and **off-chain computation frameworks** for heavy processing.

Integrating IPFS and Arweave for Data Storage

Blockchain applications require **decentralized, secure, and efficient data storage**. While blockchains provide **immutability and transparency**, they are not designed for storing **large amounts of data** due to **high costs and network constraints**. This is where **decentralized storage networks** like **IPFS (InterPlanetary File System) and Arweave** come in.

By integrating **IPFS and Arweave**, developers can store **large files, metadata, and application states** while maintaining **data persistence, security, and accessibility** without relying on centralized servers.

Why Use Decentralized Storage?

Traditional cloud storage solutions such as **Amazon S3, Google Drive, and Dropbox** are **centralized**, meaning:

Users must **trust a third party** to keep their data accessible.

Files can be **censored, deleted, or modified**.

Downtime or service failures **affect accessibility**.

Decentralized storage networks solve these problems by ensuring:

Censorship resistance – No single entity controls stored data.

Data permanence – Content remains available even if some nodes go offline.

Cost efficiency – Users only pay once for permanent storage (Arweave) or store data in a peer-to-peer manner (IPFS).

Storing and Retrieving Data Using IPFS

How IPFS Works

IPFS is a **peer-to-peer distributed file storage network** where files are stored **based on content addressing** rather than location-based addressing (e.g., URLs).

When a file is uploaded to IPFS, it receives a **Content Identifier (CID)**, a unique cryptographic hash that represents the file's contents. This CID can be **shared, stored on a blockchain, or retrieved later** without relying on centralized servers.

Uploading Files to IPFS in Rust

To interact with IPFS using Rust, install the `ipfs-api` crate:

```
[dependencies]
ipfs-api = "0.9"
tokio = { version = "1", features = ["full"] }
```

Create a Rust function to upload a file to an IPFS node:

```rust
use ipfs_api::IpfsClient;
use tokio::fs::File;
use tokio::io::AsyncReadExt;

#[tokio::main]
async fn main() {
    let client = IpfsClient::default();

    let mut file =
File::open("example.txt").await.expect("Failed to
open file");
    let mut buffer = Vec::new();
    file.read_to_end(&mut
buffer).await.expect("Failed to read file");
```

172

```rust
    match client.add(buffer).await {
        Ok(response) => println!("File uploaded to
IPFS. CID: {}", response.hash),
        Err(e) => eprintln!("Error uploading file:
{}", e),
    }
}
```

Retrieving Files from IPFS in Rust

Once a file is uploaded, retrieve it using its CID:

```rust
use ipfs_api::IpfsClient;
use tokio::io::AsyncWriteExt;

#[tokio::main]
async fn main() {
    let client = IpfsClient::default();
    let cid =
"QmYwAPJzv5CZsnAzt8L4R2c7yrn7YKc7z3R5B4Gpko7xMo";
// Replace with actual CID

    let data = client.cat(cid).await.expect("Failed
to retrieve file");

    let mut file =
tokio::fs::File::create("retrieved.txt").await.expe
ct("Failed to create file");
    file.write_all(&data).await.expect("Failed to
write file");

    println!("File retrieved and saved as
retrieved.txt");
}
```

Uploading Files to IPFS in JavaScript

For frontend applications, use `ipfs-http-client`:

```
npm install ipfs-http-client
```
Then, upload a file:

```javascript
import { create } from "ipfs-http-client";
```

```
const ipfs = create({ host: "ipfs.infura.io", port:
5001, protocol: "https" });

async function uploadToIPFS(file) {
    const added = await ipfs.add(file);
    console.log("File uploaded to IPFS. CID:",
added.path);
}
```

This allows **web applications** to upload files directly to IPFS, making them accessible **from any node in the network**.

Storing Files Permanently on Arweave

How Arweave Works

Arweave is a **permanent, decentralized storage network** that allows users to store data **forever** with a single upfront fee. Unlike IPFS, which requires **pinning services** to keep data available, Arweave guarantees **permanent storage** by using a blockchain-based economic model.

When a file is uploaded to Arweave, it is stored **across multiple nodes** and assigned a **permanent transaction ID**. This ID can be used to retrieve the file at any time, ensuring **long-term availability**.

Uploading Files to Arweave in JavaScript

To interact with Arweave, install `arweave`:

```
npm install arweave
```

Upload a file using JavaScript:

```
import Arweave from "arweave";

const arweave = Arweave.init({ host: "arweave.net",
protocol: "https" });

async function uploadToArweave(file) {
    const data = await file.arrayBuffer();
    const transaction = await
arweave.createTransaction({ data });
    await arweave.transactions.sign(transaction);
    await arweave.transactions.post(transaction);
```

```
    console.log("File stored at:",
`https://arweave.net/${transaction.id}`);
}
```
This stores the file **permanently** and generates a link such as:

```
https://arweave.net/txid
```

Retrieving Files from Arweave

To retrieve a file, simply use its **transaction ID**:

```
async function fetchFromArweave(txid) {
    const response = await
fetch(`https://arweave.net/${txid}`);
    const data = await response.text();
    console.log("Retrieved file content:", data);
}
```

This makes **Arweave ideal** for applications requiring **long-term storage of NFTs, documents, and archives**.

Integrating IPFS and Arweave with Smart Contracts

Storing IPFS CIDs on Ethereum Smart Contracts

Instead of storing entire files on Ethereum, store only their **IPFS CIDs** in a smart contract:

```
pragma solidity ^0.8.0;

contract IPFSStorage {
    mapping(uint256 => string) public fileRecords;
    uint256 public fileCount;

    function storeFile(string memory cid) public {
        fileCount++;
        fileRecords[fileCount] = cid;
    }

    function retrieveFile(uint256 fileId) public
view returns (string memory) {
        return fileRecords[fileId];
    }
}
```

Using Arweave in Smart Contracts

For permanent storage, store **Arweave transaction IDs** instead of CIDs:

```solidity
pragma solidity ^0.8.0;

contract ArweaveStorage {
    mapping(uint256 => string) public files;
    uint256 public fileCounter;

    function addFile(string memory arweaveTxId)
public {
        fileCounter++;
        files[fileCounter] = arweaveTxId;
    }

    function getFile(uint256 fileId) public view
returns (string memory) {
        return files[fileId];
    }
}
```

Users can **upload files to IPFS or Arweave** and store the **content hashes or transaction IDs** on a blockchain, ensuring **decentralized file access without bloating on-chain storage**.

By integrating **IPFS and Arweave**, developers can build **truly decentralized applications** that store and retrieve data **efficiently and securely** without relying on centralized servers.

Use IPFS for dynamic content and temporary storage.

Use Arweave for permanent, long-term storage.

Combine these solutions with smart contracts to enable **fully decentralized applications** that are scalable, cost-efficient, and resilient against data loss.

With these tools, applications can **store files, NFTs, and metadata trustlessly**, ensuring **decentralization and accessibility for future generations**.

Off-Chain Computation with Rust

Blockchain networks offer transparency, security, and immutability, but they come with significant limitations, particularly when it comes to **computational efficiency and cost**. On-chain computations, such as executing complex smart contracts, require **gas fees**, are **limited in processing power**, and **must remain deterministic**.

Off-chain computation addresses these challenges by **performing heavy processing outside the blockchain** while ensuring that results remain **verifiable, secure, and tamper-resistant**. Rust, known for its **high performance, memory safety, and concurrency model**, is an excellent choice for building **off-chain computing solutions** that interact seamlessly with blockchains.

Why Off-Chain Computation is Necessary

Blockchains are **not designed** for performing intensive computations due to:

Gas Costs: Every on-chain operation requires computational power, which must be paid for in gas fees. Complex calculations can become prohibitively expensive.

Limited Execution Time: Smart contracts must execute within a strict time frame; long-running operations may fail due to gas exhaustion.

Deterministic Execution: Smart contract computations must produce the same result every time they run, limiting randomness and advanced processing.

Off-chain computation allows developers to:

Run complex calculations off-chain and store only the results on-chain.

Use secure cryptographic proofs to verify off-chain execution.

Leverage Rust's concurrency to process blockchain data efficiently.

Building a Rust Off-Chain Computation Service

A **Rust off-chain service** can process data, perform computations, and interact with a blockchain by **submitting results to smart contracts**. Let's build a **Rust API that calculates the sum of a list of numbers** and submits it to an Ethereum smart contract.

Step 1: Setting Up the Rust Project

Create a new Rust project:

```
cargo new rust_offchain_computation
cd rust_offchain_computation
```

Modify `Cargo.toml` to include dependencies:

```
[dependencies]
warp = "0.3"
serde = { version = "1.0", features = ["derive"] }
serde_json = "1.0"
tokio = { version = "1", features = ["full"] }
ethers = "2.0"
```

`warp`: A fast web framework for building Rust APIs.

`serde`: Enables JSON serialization and deserialization.

`tokio`: Provides async runtime for handling concurrent requests.

`ethers`: Allows interaction with Ethereum smart contracts.

Step 2: Implementing Off-Chain Computation in Rust

Create a simple API that accepts a list of numbers, computes their sum, and returns the result.

Modify `src/main.rs`:

```
use warp::Filter;
use serde::{Serialize, Deserialize};
use ethers::prelude::*;
use std::sync::Arc;

#[derive(Serialize, Deserialize)]
struct ComputationRequest {
    numbers: Vec<u64>,
}

#[derive(Serialize)]
struct ComputationResponse {
    result: u64,
```

```
}

async fn compute_sum(req: ComputationRequest) ->
warp::reply::Json {
    let sum: u64 = req.numbers.iter().sum();
    warp::reply::json(&ComputationResponse {
result: sum })
}

#[tokio::main]
async fn main() {
    let compute_route = warp::post()
        .and(warp::path("compute"))
        .and(warp::body::json())
        .map(compute_sum);

    warp::serve(compute_route).run(([127, 0, 0, 1],
8080)).await;
}
```

How it Works:

The API listens for POST requests at /compute.

It expects a JSON payload containing an array of numbers.

It computes the sum and returns the result as JSON.

Step 3: Running the Rust API

Compile and run the server:

`cargo run`

Send a request to compute the sum of [3, 5, 7]:

```
curl -X POST http://127.0.0.1:8080/compute -H
"Content-Type: application/json" -d '{"numbers":
[3,5,7]}'
```

Expected response:

```
{
    "result": 15
}
```

Submitting Off-Chain Computation Results to a Smart Contract

Now that we have computed a result off-chain, we need to **send it to an Ethereum smart contract** for verification.

Step 1: Deploy a Smart Contract to Store Computation Results

Create a Solidity contract:

```solidity
pragma solidity ^0.8.0;

contract OffChainComputation {
    uint256 public lastComputedSum;

    function storeResult(uint256 _result) public {
        lastComputedSum = _result;
    }
}
```

Deploy this contract on a **local Ethereum testnet (Ganache) or a public network (Goerli, Sepolia).**

Step 2: Submit Computation Results from Rust

Modify `src/main.rs` to include Ethereum interaction:

```rust
async fn submit_to_contract(result: u64) ->
Result<(), Box<dyn std::error::Error>> {
    let provider =
Provider::<Http>::try_from("https://goerli.infura.io/v3/YOUR_INFURA_KEY")?;
    let wallet =
"YOUR_PRIVATE_KEY".parse::<LocalWallet>()?;
    let client = SignerMiddleware::new(provider,
wallet);

    let contract_address: Address =
"0xYourContractAddress".parse()?;
    let abi = include_bytes!("contract_abi.json");
// Load ABI

    let contract = Contract::from_json(client,
contract_address, abi)?;
```

```
    let tx = contract.method::<_,
H256>("storeResult", result)?.send().await?;
    println!("Transaction Hash: {:?}", tx);

    Ok(())
}
```

This function:

Connects to an Ethereum RPC provider.

Loads the smart contract using its ABI and address.

Calls `storeResult()` to store the computed sum on-chain.

Zero-Knowledge Proofs (ZKPs) for Off-Chain Computation

Zero-Knowledge Proofs (**ZKPs**) allow verification of off-chain computations **without revealing sensitive data**. This is useful in **privacy-focused** applications such as:

Private transaction validation.

Proving identity without revealing credentials.

Secure multiparty computations.

Using Rust for Zero-Knowledge Proofs (ZK-SNARKs)

Install the `bellman` crate:

```
[dependencies]
bellman = { git =
"https://github.com/zkcrypto/bellman" }
rand = "0.8"
```

Implement a **basic zero-knowledge proof**:

```
use bellman::groth16::{create_random_proof,
verify_proof, Parameters};
use rand::rngs::OsRng;

fn generate_proof() {
    let params =
Parameters::generate_random::<Bls12, _>(OsRng);
```

```
    let proof = create_random_proof(params,
OsRng).unwrap();
    println!("Generated Zero-Knowledge Proof:
{:?}", proof);
}
```

ZKPs ensure that **off-chain computations are verifiable** without requiring all computations to be done **on-chain**.

Real-World Applications of Rust-Based Off-Chain Computation

Optimized NFT Metadata Processing

An NFT marketplace uses Rust to **precompute** metadata hashes **off-chain** before storing the hash on-chain.

Verifiable Machine Learning

A decentralized AI system runs deep-learning models in Rust, **submits results** to a blockchain, and proves correctness with ZKPs.

Financial Computations for DeFi

A DeFi protocol runs **risk assessment models** off-chain in Rust and commits final calculations **to an Ethereum contract**.

Rust is an ideal language for **off-chain computation** due to its **speed, safety, and concurrency support**. By **processing data off-chain and submitting verified results on-chain**, developers can:

Reduce gas costs by avoiding expensive on-chain operations.

Scale blockchain applications without overloading network nodes.

Improve security and privacy using Zero-Knowledge Proofs.

With Rust-powered **off-chain computation services**, developers can **optimize blockchain applications**, ensuring they are **efficient, scalable, and cost-effective**.

Using Oracles and Zero-Knowledge Proofs

182

Blockchain technology provides **security, decentralization, and transparency**, but it operates in a **closed system**—meaning that **smart contracts cannot access external data** on their own. This limitation makes it challenging for **decentralized applications (DApps)** to incorporate real-world information, such as **weather data, stock prices, sports scores, or election results**.

To bridge this gap, developers use **oracles**—services that fetch **off-chain data** and submit it to **on-chain smart contracts** in a **secure and verifiable** manner.

Additionally, **Zero-Knowledge Proofs (ZKPs)** enable blockchains to perform **privacy-preserving verifications** without revealing sensitive information. This is useful for **identity verification, financial transactions, and secure multiparty computations**.

Blockchains **cannot** fetch data from external sources because they are **deterministic systems**. This means every transaction and computation on a blockchain must be **reproducible by all network nodes** to maintain consensus.

However, many decentralized applications require **real-world data**, such as:

DeFi protocols needing real-time **crypto exchange rates**.

Insurance smart contracts requiring weather conditions for **claim validation**.

NFT-based gaming using real-world **sports scores** to determine in-game rewards.

How Oracles Work

An oracle is a **middleware service** that fetches, verifies, and submits **off-chain data to on-chain smart contracts**.

The process typically follows these steps:

Request: A smart contract **asks the oracle for external data**.

Fetch: The oracle retrieves the data from an **API, website, or IoT device**.

Validate: The oracle ensures the data is **accurate and tamper-proof**.

183

Submit: The oracle **transmits the data** to the smart contract.

Some popular oracle networks include:

Chainlink (decentralized, widely used).

Band Protocol (cross-chain oracle).

API3 (first-party oracles).

Implementing a Rust-Based Oracle with Chainlink

Chainlink is the **most widely used decentralized oracle network**. It allows smart contracts to fetch **off-chain data** in a trust-minimized way.

Step 1: Deploying a Smart Contract to Request Data from Chainlink

The following **Solidity contract** retrieves the **ETH/USD price** from Chainlink's on-chain price feed:

```solidity
pragma solidity ^0.8.0;

import
"@chainlink/contracts/src/v0.8/interfaces/Aggregato
rV3Interface.sol";

contract PriceOracle {
    AggregatorV3Interface internal priceFeed;

    constructor() {
        // Chainlink's ETH/USD price feed on
Ethereum mainnet
        priceFeed =
AggregatorV3Interface(0x5f4ec3df9cbd43714fe2740f5e3
616155c5b8419);
    }

    function getLatestPrice() public view returns
(int) {
        (, int price, , , ) =
priceFeed.latestRoundData();
        return price;
    }
```

```
}
```

Step 2: Fetching Oracle Data Using Rust

To interact with the smart contract from a Rust backend, install the `ethers` crate:

```
[dependencies]
ethers = "2.0"
tokio = { version = "1", features = ["full"] }
```

Then, implement a Rust function to read the latest price:

```
use ethers::prelude::*;
use std::sync::Arc;

#[tokio::main]
async fn main() -> eyre::Result<()> {
    let provider =
Provider::<Http>::try_from("https://mainnet.infura.
io/v3/YOUR_INFURA_KEY")?;
    let contract_address: Address =
"0x5f4ec3df9cbd43714fe2740f5e3616155c5b8419".parse(
)?;
    let abi = include_bytes!("chainlink_abi.json");

    let contract = Contract::from_json(provider,
contract_address, abi)?;
    let price: i64 =
contract.method("getLatestPrice",
())?.call().await?;

    println!("ETH/USD Price: {}", price);

    Ok(())
}
```

Step 3: Submitting Oracle Data to a Smart Contract

If off-chain data needs to be **pushed to a blockchain**, modify the Rust service to submit a transaction:

```
use ethers::signers::Wallet;
use ethers::types::TransactionRequest;

#[tokio::main]
```

```
async fn main() -> eyre::Result<()> {
    let provider =
Provider::<Http>::try_from("https://mainnet.infura.
io/v3/YOUR_INFURA_KEY")?;
    let wallet =
"YOUR_PRIVATE_KEY".parse::<Wallet>()?;
    let client = SignerMiddleware::new(provider,
wallet);

    let contract_address: Address =
"0xYourContractAddress".parse()?;
    let abi = include_bytes!("contract_abi.json");

    let contract = Contract::from_json(client,
contract_address, abi)?;

    let price: i64 = 3200; // Fetch from external
source
    let tx = contract.method::<_,
H256>("storePrice", price)?.send().await?;

    println!("Transaction submitted: {:?}", tx);

    Ok(())
}
```

This allows **any Rust application** to fetch external data and submit it to a blockchain.

Zero-Knowledge Proofs (ZKPs) for Privacy and Security

A **Zero-Knowledge Proof (ZKP)** is a cryptographic method that allows one party to **prove a statement is true without revealing the actual data**.

ZKPs enable:

Anonymous identity verification without exposing personal details.

Privacy-preserving transactions in blockchain payments.

Scalable blockchain computations (ZK-Rollups in Ethereum Layer 2).

Types of ZKPs

ZK-SNARKs (Succinct Non-Interactive Argument of Knowledge)

186

Short proof size and fast verification.

Used in **Zcash for private transactions**.

ZK-STARKs (Scalable Transparent Argument of Knowledge)

No trusted setup, more scalable than SNARKs.

Implementing Zero-Knowledge Proofs in Rust

Rust supports **ZKPs** using cryptographic libraries such as `bellman` for ZK-SNARKs.

Step 1: Install the Bellman Library

Add the dependency:

```
[dependencies]
bellman = { git =
"https://github.com/zkcrypto/bellman" }
rand = "0.8"
```

Step 2: Generate a Zero-Knowledge Proof

The following Rust code generates a **ZK-SNARK proof**:

```
use bellman::groth16::{create_random_proof,
verify_proof, Parameters};
use rand::rngs::OsRng;

fn generate_proof() {
    let params =
Parameters::generate_random::<Bls12, _>(OsRng);
    let proof = create_random_proof(params,
OsRng).unwrap();
    println!("Generated ZK Proof: {:?}", proof);
}
```

Step 3: Verify a Zero-Knowledge Proof

```
fn verify_proof(proof: Proof<Bls12>) -> bool {
    let params =
Parameters::generate_random::<Bls12, _>(OsRng);
    verify_proof(params.vk, &proof, &[]).is_ok()
}
```

187

Zero-Knowledge Proofs allow **off-chain computations to be verified on-chain** without revealing private data.

Oracles and Zero-Knowledge Proofs are **critical tools** for enabling **secure, scalable, and private blockchain applications**.

Oracles allow blockchains to fetch **real-world data**, making **DeFi, supply chains, and insurance applications possible**.

ZKPs ensure privacy by allowing users to **prove information without revealing sensitive details**.

By integrating **Rust-powered Oracles and ZKPs**, developers can build **decentralized, trustless, and privacy-preserving applications** while maintaining **efficiency, scalability, and security**.

Chapter 10: Blockchain Consensus Mechanisms

A blockchain is a distributed ledger where multiple participants maintain a shared state **without trusting each other**. To ensure **consistency, security, and immutability**, blockchains use **consensus mechanisms**—protocols that allow nodes to **agree on the state of the network**.

Consensus mechanisms play a crucial role in determining:

How transactions are validated.

How blocks are added to the chain.

How malicious actors are prevented from corrupting the system.

Rust, with its **high performance, memory safety, and concurrency model**, is widely used in the development of blockchain consensus mechanisms. This chapter explores:

How different consensus mechanisms work (PoW, PoS, DPoS, etc.).

How Rust contributes to consensus implementations.

How to implement a basic consensus algorithm in Rust.

Overview of PoW, PoS, DPoS, and Other Models

Blockchain networks rely on **consensus mechanisms** to ensure that all participants agree on the state of the ledger. A consensus mechanism is a protocol that determines how transactions are validated and added to the blockchain **without requiring trust** between parties.

Different blockchain networks use different consensus models, each designed to balance **security, decentralization, and efficiency**. The most widely used models are **Proof of Work (PoW), Proof of Stake (PoS), and Delegated Proof of Stake (DPoS)**, along with several newer variations.

189

This section provides a clear and detailed explanation of these models, their advantages, disadvantages, and real-world applications.

Proof of Work (PoW)

Proof of Work (PoW) is the **original** blockchain consensus mechanism, introduced by **Bitcoin** in 2009. It relies on **computational power** to validate transactions and secure the network.

Miners compete to solve a complex mathematical puzzle by finding a special number called a **nonce**.

This process involves repeatedly hashing a block's data until the output meets a specific difficulty requirement.

The first miner to solve the puzzle **broadcasts the solution** to the network.

Other nodes verify the solution and, if valid, the new block is added to the blockchain.

The winning miner receives a **block reward** plus transaction fees.

This process, called **mining**, ensures that only **honest nodes** contribute to the blockchain, since attempting to modify past transactions would require an impractical amount of computational power.

Advantages of PoW

Highly Secure: PoW is resistant to **Sybil attacks** (where an attacker creates multiple fake identities) because gaining majority control would require owning most of the network's computing power.

Decentralized: Anyone can participate in mining, making it difficult for a single entity to control the network.

Immutable Transactions: Once a block is added, altering it would require re-mining all subsequent blocks, making attacks extremely expensive.

Disadvantages of PoW

Energy-Intensive: Mining consumes a large amount of electricity, making PoW less sustainable.

Slow Transactions: Bitcoin's PoW mechanism limits scalability, processing only about **7 transactions per second (TPS)**.

High Costs: Specialized mining hardware (ASICs) makes it expensive for individuals to participate.

Real-World Examples

Bitcoin (BTC) – The first and most well-known PoW blockchain.

Ethereum (ETH) – Used PoW before switching to PoS in 2022.

Litecoin (LTC) – A PoW network with faster block times than Bitcoin.

Proof of Stake (PoS)

Proof of Stake (PoS) is a consensus mechanism that selects **validators** based on the amount of cryptocurrency they **stake** as collateral. Instead of competing through computational work, validators are chosen **randomly** based on their stake.

Users **lock up** (stake) a certain amount of cryptocurrency in the network.

The protocol selects **validators** based on the size of their stake and a randomization process.

Chosen validators **propose and validate new blocks**.

Validators earn rewards, but if they act dishonestly, they **lose part of their stake** (a process called **slashing**).

Advantages of PoS

Energy-Efficient: Unlike PoW, PoS does not require mining, reducing power consumption by over **99%**.

Faster Transactions: PoS networks handle more transactions per second (Ethereum 2.0 can process **100,000+ TPS** with sharding).

Lower Costs: Staking does not require expensive mining hardware, making it accessible to more users.

Disadvantages of PoS

Risk of Centralization: Wealthier participants who stake more tokens have a higher chance of being chosen as validators.

Long-Range Attacks: If attackers control old private keys, they could rewrite blockchain history.

Real-World Examples

Ethereum 2.0 (ETH) – Moved from PoW to PoS for greater efficiency.

Cardano (ADA) – Uses **Ouroboros**, a secure PoS protocol.

Polkadot (DOT) – Uses **Nominated Proof of Stake (NPoS)** for validator selection.

Delegated Proof of Stake (DPoS)

Delegated Proof of Stake (DPoS) is a variation of PoS where token holders **vote for a small number of delegates** to validate transactions on their behalf.

Users **vote for trusted validators** (also called delegates) based on the number of tokens they hold.

The top validators (usually 21–100) are responsible for confirming transactions and creating new blocks.

Validators receive rewards and distribute a portion to their supporters (voters).

If a validator acts maliciously, voters can **replace them**.

Advantages of DPoS

Highly Scalable: With fewer validators, DPoS achieves faster transaction speeds (**EOS processes over 4,000 TPS**).

More Democratic: Users have direct voting power over network governance.

Lower Energy Costs: Does not require mining.

Disadvantages of DPoS

Potential Centralization: A small number of delegates control the network.

Voter Apathy: If users don't participate in voting, large stakeholders can dominate the system.

Real-World Examples

EOS (EOS) – One of the first blockchains to implement DPoS.

Tron (TRX) – Uses **Super Representatives** (top 27 voted delegates).

Steem (STEEM) – A social blockchain that uses DPoS.

Other Consensus Models

Proof of Authority (PoA)

Validators are **pre-approved** and known entities.

Used in **private blockchains** where security is not a major concern.

Example: **VeChain (VET), Binance Smart Chain (BSC)**.

Proof of Burn (PoB)

Users **destroy (burn) coins** to gain mining power.

More burned coins increase mining eligibility.

Example: **Slimcoin** (a lesser-known PoB blockchain).

Proof of History (PoH)

Used in **Solana**, PoH timestamps transactions **before consensus** to increase speed.

Allows **50,000+ TPS**, much faster than PoS or PoW.

Hybrid Models

Nominated Proof of Stake (NPoS): Used in **Polkadot**, combines **PoS with community voting** for validator selection.

Leased Proof of Stake (LPoS): Used in **Waves**, where users can lease tokens to validators.

Choosing the Right Consensus Model

Each consensus mechanism is designed for different **use cases**:

PoW is best for **security-focused, decentralized** blockchains (e.g., Bitcoin).

193

PoS is best for **scalable, eco-friendly** networks (e.g., Ethereum 2.0, Cardano).

DPoS is best for **high-speed applications** with governance features (e.g., EOS, Tron).

PoA and hybrid models are useful for **enterprise and private blockchains**.

Understanding these mechanisms is essential for **blockchain developers, investors, and users** to evaluate the strengths and trade-offs of different networks. As the blockchain industry evolves, **hybrid and innovative models** will continue to emerge, improving scalability, efficiency, and security.

How Rust is Used in Consensus Mechanisms

Consensus mechanisms are the **foundation of blockchain networks**, ensuring that all participants agree on the state of transactions **without relying on a central authority**. These mechanisms must be **fast, secure, and efficient** to support large-scale blockchain operations.

Rust plays a crucial role in **building consensus mechanisms** due to its:

High performance – Rust compiles to efficient machine code, allowing consensus mechanisms to process transactions with minimal latency.

Memory safety – Prevents vulnerabilities like **buffer overflows and memory leaks**, reducing attack vectors.

Concurrency model – Uses **async programming** and **actor-based frameworks** to process multiple transactions in parallel, which is critical for blockchain scalability.

Rust is widely adopted in **leading blockchain projects**, including **Polkadot, Solana, and Ethereum 2.0**. It is used to implement **custom consensus algorithms, network synchronization, and state validation** in high-performance blockchain systems.

Why Rust is Preferred for Consensus Mechanisms

Performance and Low-Level Control

Consensus algorithms require **fast and predictable execution** to handle thousands of transactions per second. Rust provides **zero-cost abstractions**, meaning developers get high-level safety guarantees **without sacrificing speed**.

In contrast, languages like **Python and JavaScript** introduce **garbage collection pauses**, which can slow down transaction finalization in a distributed blockchain network. Rust eliminates this problem **by managing memory at compile time**, ensuring consistent execution times.

Memory Safety Without Garbage Collection

Memory-related bugs, such as **buffer overflows and null pointer dereferences**, are common attack vectors in blockchain software. Rust **prevents these issues at compile time**, making consensus mechanisms **more resistant to exploits** like:

Reentrancy attacks, where a malicious contract drains funds by repeatedly calling a function before the first execution completes.

Use-after-free errors, which can cause unpredictable behavior in smart contracts and consensus validation.

With Rust's **ownership system**, variables follow strict rules, ensuring that data cannot be **mutated unexpectedly**, reducing security risks.

Concurrency for Large-Scale Blockchain Networks

Consensus mechanisms involve **multiple nodes processing transactions simultaneously**, requiring **efficient thread management**. Rust's **async runtime** (Tokio or async-std) allows nodes to process **thousands of transactions concurrently** without blocking execution.

In contrast, languages like **Go** or **Java** require a **garbage collector**, which can introduce performance bottlenecks when processing large transaction volumes.

Real-World Blockchain Projects Using Rust for Consensus

Polkadot: Nominated Proof of Stake (NPoS) with Substrate

Polkadot uses **Nominated Proof of Stake (NPoS)**, where token holders **nominate validators** to secure the network. This model requires an **efficient validator selection process**, which is implemented in Rust using **Substrate**— a Rust-based blockchain framework.

Example: Validator election logic in Substrate (Rust-based consensus engine):

```
use sp_std::vec::Vec;
use sp_runtime::traits::{Zero, One};

/// A simple election algorithm to select top
validators based on stake
fn select_validators(candidates: Vec<(u64, u128)>,
num_validators: u64) -> Vec<u64> {
    let mut sorted_candidates = candidates;
    sorted_candidates.sort_by(|a, b|
b.1.cmp(&a.1)); // Sort by stake (descending)
    sorted_candidates.iter().take(num_validators as
usize).map(|(id, _)| *id).collect()
}
```

This function selects validators **based on the highest stake**, ensuring **a fair and decentralized election process**.

Solana: Proof of History (PoH) with Rust for High-Speed Consensus

Solana uses **Proof of History (PoH)**, which timestamps transactions **before consensus**, allowing nodes to **agree on order without waiting for confirmations**.

Rust is used to implement **Solana's transaction processing pipeline**, handling **50,000+ transactions per second** with low latency.

Example: Solana's Rust-based PoH implementation for timestamping transactions:

```
use sha2::{Sha256, Digest};

/// Generates a Proof of History hash chain
fn generate_poh(previous_hash: &str, data: &str) ->
String {
    let mut hasher = Sha256::new();
```

```
    hasher.update(previous_hash);
    hasher.update(data);
    format!("{:x}", hasher.finalize())
}
```

This function continuously **hashes previous values**, creating an **unforgeable sequence of timestamps**.

Implementing a Simple Consensus Algorithm in Rust

Let's build a **basic Proof of Work (PoW) consensus mechanism** in Rust. This example simulates **mining** by solving a cryptographic puzzle.

Step 1: Define the Block Structure

Modify `src/main.rs` to define a **block** containing transaction data and a proof-of-work solution.

```rust
use sha2::{Sha256, Digest};
use std::time::{SystemTime, UNIX_EPOCH};

#[derive(Debug)]
struct Block {
    index: u64,
    timestamp: u128,
    data: String,
    previous_hash: String,
    nonce: u64,
    hash: String,
}

impl Block {
    fn new(index: u64, data: String, previous_hash:
String) -> Self {
        let timestamp = SystemTime::now()
            .duration_since(UNIX_EPOCH)
            .unwrap()
            .as_millis();

        let mut nonce = 0;
        let mut hash = String::new();

        while !hash.starts_with("0000") {  //
Adjust difficulty by changing zeros
```

```
                    nonce += 1;
                    let input = format!("{}{}{}{}{}",
index, timestamp, &data, &previous_hash, nonce);
                    hash = format!("{:x}",
Sha256::digest(input.as_bytes()));
            }

            Block {
                index,
                timestamp,
                data,
                previous_hash,
                nonce,
                hash,
            }
        }
}
```

This **mines a block** by finding a hash that meets a **difficulty requirement** (leading zeros).

Step 2: Implement the Blockchain Structure

Add functions to manage a blockchain and **validate new blocks**.

```
struct Blockchain {
    chain: Vec<Block>,
}

impl Blockchain {
    fn new() -> Self {
        Blockchain {
            chain: vec![Block::new(0, "Genesis
Block".to_string(), "0".to_string())],
        }
    }

    fn add_block(&mut self, data: String) {
        let previous_hash =
self.chain.last().unwrap().hash.clone();
        let new_block = Block::new(self.chain.len()
as u64, data, previous_hash);
        self.chain.push(new_block);
    }
```

```
    fn print_chain(&self) {
        for block in &self.chain {
            println!("{:?}", block);
        }
    }
}

fn main() {
    let mut blockchain = Blockchain::new();

    blockchain.add_block("Transaction: Alice ->
Bob: 10 BTC".to_string());
    blockchain.add_block("Transaction: Bob ->
Charlie: 5 BTC".to_string());

    blockchain.print_chain();
}
```

Step 3: Running the Rust-Based Consensus Algorithm

Compile and run:

cargo run

Expected output:

```
Block { index: 1, data: "Transaction: Alice -> Bob:
10 BTC", nonce: 10312, hash: "0000abcd..." }
Block { index: 2, data: "Transaction: Bob ->
Charlie: 5 BTC", nonce: 45289, hash: "0000efgh..."
}
```

Each block is mined by **finding a hash with a leading "0000"**, simulating **Proof of Work**.

Rust is an **ideal language** for developing **blockchain consensus mechanisms** due to its **speed, memory safety, and concurrency support**. It is widely used in:

PoS-based networks (Polkadot, Ethereum 2.0) to manage validator elections.

High-speed networks (Solana, Near Protocol) that process thousands of transactions per second.

Custom consensus mechanisms where **low-level control and security** are essential.

With Rust-powered consensus engines, blockchain networks can achieve **scalability, efficiency, and security**, ensuring a **robust decentralized system**.

Implementing a Simple Consensus Algorithm in Rust

Consensus mechanisms are at the core of blockchain networks, ensuring that all participants agree on the state of the ledger **without relying on a central authority**. These mechanisms must be **secure, efficient, and resistant to attacks** to maintain the integrity of the system.

Rust is an excellent language for building consensus algorithms because it provides **high performance, memory safety, and concurrency support**, making it ideal for **secure and scalable blockchain development**.

A consensus algorithm ensures that all nodes in a blockchain network agree on **which transactions are valid** and **which blocks should be added** to the chain.

In a **Proof of Work (PoW)** system, nodes (miners) **compete to solve a cryptographic puzzle**. The first to solve it **proposes a new block**, and other nodes verify its validity before adding it to the chain.

The process follows these steps:

A miner selects pending transactions and forms a new block.

The miner **computes a hash** of the block data that meets a difficulty requirement (e.g., it must start with a certain number of leading zeros).

If the miner finds a valid hash, they broadcast the block to the network.

Other nodes **verify the hash** and check the block's validity.

If valid, the block is **added to the blockchain**.

This process makes blockchains **secure and immutable** because altering past transactions would require **re-mining all subsequent blocks**, which is computationally infeasible.

Implementing a Proof of Work Blockchain in Rust

Now, let's build a **simple Rust-based blockchain** with a **Proof of Work consensus algorithm**. This implementation will:

Define a **block structure** with cryptographic hashing.

Implement **mining logic** to validate new blocks.

Maintain a **blockchain with block validation**.

Step 1: Setting Up the Rust Project

First, create a new Rust project for the blockchain:

```
cargo new rust_blockchain
cd rust_blockchain
```

Edit `Cargo.toml` to include the required dependencies:

```
[dependencies]
sha2 = "0.10"   # For SHA-256 hashing
hex = "0.4"     # For encoding hashes
```

These dependencies will be used for **hashing block data** and formatting outputs.

Step 2: Creating the Block Structure

Modify `src/main.rs` to define the structure of a block:

```
use sha2::{Sha256, Digest};
use std::time::{SystemTime, UNIX_EPOCH};

#[derive(Debug)]
struct Block {
    index: u64,
    timestamp: u128,
    data: String,
    previous_hash: String,
    nonce: u64,
    hash: String,
```

```rust
}

impl Block {
    fn new(index: u64, data: String, previous_hash:
String) -> Self {
        let timestamp = SystemTime::now()
            .duration_since(UNIX_EPOCH)
            .unwrap()
            .as_millis();

        let mut nonce = 0;
        let mut hash = String::new();

        // Proof of Work: Find a hash that starts
with "0000"
        while !hash.starts_with("0000") {
            nonce += 1;
            let input = format!("{}{}{}{}{}",
index, timestamp, &data, &previous_hash, nonce);
            hash = format!("{:x}",
Sha256::digest(input.as_bytes()));
        }

        Block {
            index,
            timestamp,
            data,
            previous_hash,
            nonce,
            hash,
        }
    }
}
```

How This Works:

Each block stores **transaction data, a timestamp, the previous block's hash, and a nonce**.

The **Proof of Work function** continuously hashes the block's data until it finds a **valid hash** that starts with "0000".

The difficulty level is determined by the number of leading zeros required in the hash.

Step 3: Implementing the Blockchain Structure

Now, define a **blockchain that manages blocks and enforces consensus rules**.

Add the following to `src/main.rs`:

```
struct Blockchain {
    chain: Vec<Block>,
}

impl Blockchain {
    fn new() -> Self {
        Blockchain {
            chain: vec![Block::new(0, "Genesis
Block".to_string(), "0".to_string())],
        }
    }

    fn add_block(&mut self, data: String) {
        let previous_hash =
self.chain.last().unwrap().hash.clone();
        let new_block = Block::new(self.chain.len()
as u64, data, previous_hash);
        self.chain.push(new_block);
    }

    fn validate_chain(&self) -> bool {
        for i in 1..self.chain.len() {
            let current_block = &self.chain[i];
            let previous_block = &self.chain[i -
1];

            // Recompute the hash and check
validity
            let mut hasher = Sha256::new();
            hasher.update(format!(
                "{}{}{}{}{}",
                current_block.index,
                current_block.timestamp,
```

```
                current_block.data,
                previous_block.hash,
                current_block.nonce
            ));
            let recalculated_hash = format!("{:x}",
hasher.finalize());

            if recalculated_hash !=
current_block.hash || current_block.previous_hash
!= previous_block.hash {
                return false;
            }
        }
        true
    }

    fn print_chain(&self) {
        for block in &self.chain {
            println!("{:?}", block);
        }
    }
}
```

How This Works:

The blockchain starts with a Genesis block (index 0).

New blocks are mined and added to the chain, maintaining the hash link.

The validate_chain() function checks that all blocks **follow PoW rules** and that hashes match.

Step 4: Running the Rust-Based Consensus Algorithm

Finally, add a main() function to create and test the blockchain:

```
fn main() {
    let mut blockchain = Blockchain::new();

    println!("Mining block 1...");
    blockchain.add_block("Transaction: Alice -> Bob: 10
BTC".to_string());

    println!("Mining block 2...");
    blockchain.add_block("Transaction: Bob -> Charlie: 5
BTC".to_string());
```

```
    println!("\nBlockchain:");
    blockchain.print_chain();

    if blockchain.validate_chain() {
        println!("\nBlockchain is valid.");
    } else {
        println!("\nBlockchain validation failed!");
    }
}
```

Step 5: Compiling and Running the Blockchain

Run the program:

```
cargo run
```

Expected output:

```
Mining block 1...
Mining block 2...

Blockchain:
Block { index: 1, data: "Transaction: Alice -> Bob:
10 BTC", nonce: 10312, hash: "0000abcd..." }
Block { index: 2, data: "Transaction: Bob ->
Charlie: 5 BTC", nonce: 45289, hash: "0000efgh..."
}

Blockchain is valid.
```

Each block has a **valid PoW hash with "0000" at the start**, proving that **mining was successfully completed**.

This implementation demonstrates a **basic Proof of Work blockchain** built in Rust.

Key Takeaways:

Blocks are linked using cryptographic hashes, ensuring **immutability**.

Mining requires finding a valid hash (Proof of Work).

The blockchain verifies itself to prevent tampering.

Rust's speed and safety make it ideal for consensus mechanisms.

This project can be **extended** by adding **peer-to-peer networking, transaction pools, and more advanced consensus models**. With Rust, blockchain developers can build **efficient, scalable, and secure decentralized networks** that maintain integrity and decentralization.

Chapter 11: Building Custom Blockchains with Rust

Blockchain technology has evolved beyond cryptocurrency applications, enabling developers to build **custom blockchains** tailored for specific use cases. Rust has become a **leading language for blockchain development** due to its **performance, security, and concurrency model**.

Introduction to Substrate and Cosmos SDK

Blockchain technology has evolved beyond simple cryptocurrencies, allowing developers to create **custom blockchains** that are optimized for specific use cases. Instead of modifying existing blockchain networks like Bitcoin or Ethereum, developers can use **frameworks** that provide pre-built modules for consensus, governance, and state management.

Two of the most widely used blockchain frameworks are **Substrate** and **Cosmos SDK**. Both are designed to make blockchain development more accessible while offering flexibility for customization.

What is Substrate?

Substrate is a **modular blockchain framework** developed by **Parity Technologies**. It is designed to make it easy to build **custom blockchains** without writing an entire network from scratch.

Substrate powers **Polkadot**, a multi-chain network that allows different blockchains to communicate with each other. However, Substrate is not limited to Polkadot—it can be used to build **standalone blockchains** as well.

Key Features of Substrate

Modular Architecture: Developers can choose **pre-built components** (like networking, consensus, and transaction processing) or build custom logic.

Rust-Based: Written in **Rust**, ensuring high performance and security.

Forkless Upgrades: Allows blockchains to update their protocol **without hard forks** using **on-chain governance**.

Built-in Support for Proof of Stake (PoS) and Custom Consensus: Developers can implement PoS, PoW, or their own consensus mechanisms.

Polkadot Integration: Can be connected to the **Polkadot network** as a **parachain** or run as an independent blockchain.

How Substrate Works

Substrate follows a **modular approach**, meaning developers can pick and customize components based on their needs.

It consists of:

Runtime: Defines how transactions and state changes are processed. Written in **Rust and compiled to WebAssembly (Wasm)**.

FRAME (Framework for Runtime Aggregation of Modular Entities): A set of pre-built **Rust-based modules (called pallets)** that provide standard blockchain functionality, such as accounts, smart contracts, and governance.

Networking Layer: Handles communication between nodes in a decentralized network.

Consensus Layer: Manages how nodes agree on new blocks (PoW, PoS, or custom algorithms).

When to Use Substrate

Substrate is a good choice if:

You need a **highly customizable** blockchain.

You want to use **Rust** and WebAssembly for performance and security.

You need **on-chain governance and upgradeability**.

You want your blockchain to be **compatible with Polkadot** for cross-chain communication.

Example of a Simple Substrate Blockchain

To create a **new blockchain using Substrate**, install the Substrate development environment:

```
cargo install --git
https://github.com/paritytech/substrate substrate-
node
```

Run a **local blockchain node**:

```
substrate-node --dev
```

This starts a **fully functional blockchain** with accounts, transactions, and a governance system. Developers can modify the **runtime logic** by adding custom **pallets** to handle different types of transactions.

What is Cosmos SDK?

Cosmos SDK is an **open-source framework** for building **sovereign blockchains** that can communicate with each other. It is part of the **Cosmos ecosystem**, which enables interoperability between independent blockchains using the **Inter-Blockchain Communication (IBC) protocol**.

Unlike Substrate, which is tightly integrated with Polkadot, Cosmos SDK is designed for blockchains that **operate independently** while still having the ability to connect with others if needed.

Key Features of Cosmos SDK

Modular Design: Developers can **use or customize existing modules** for accounts, governance, staking, and smart contracts.

Tendermint Consensus: Uses the **Tendermint consensus engine**, which is a fast and secure **Byzantine Fault Tolerant (BFT)** mechanism.

Interoperability: Supports **cross-chain communication** via the **IBC protocol**.

Proof of Stake (PoS) by Default: Staking and validator selection are built-in.

Governance and Upgradability: Supports **on-chain voting and governance**.

Go-Based: Written in **Go**, which is simpler than Rust but may not offer the same performance guarantees.

How Cosmos SDK Works

209

Cosmos SDK blockchains are built using **two core components**:

Cosmos SDK – A framework for creating blockchain logic.

Tendermint Core – The consensus and networking engine that ensures fast finality.

A typical Cosmos-based blockchain consists of:

Base App: Defines the core blockchain logic (accounts, governance, staking).

Modules: Pre-built or custom modules that add features such as smart contracts.

IBC Protocol: Allows Cosmos-based chains to communicate with each other.

2.3 When to Use Cosmos SDK

Cosmos SDK is a good choice if:

You need a **sovereign blockchain** that operates independently.

You want **fast finality and high transaction throughput**.

You need **cross-chain interoperability** via IBC.

You prefer **Go-based development** over Rust.

2.4 Example of a Simple Cosmos SDK Blockchain

To create a **new blockchain using Cosmos SDK**, install the `ignite` CLI tool:

```
curl https://get.ignite.com/cli! | bash
```

Create a new blockchain:

```
ignite scaffold chain mychain

cd mychain

ignite chain serve
```

This launches a **local blockchain node**, with pre-configured modules for **accounts, transactions, and staking**.

Substrate vs. Cosmos SDK: Choosing the Right Framework

While both Substrate and Cosmos SDK allow developers to build custom blockchains, they **differ in architecture, design philosophy, and flexibility**.

Feature	Substrate	Cosmos SDK
Language	Rust	Go
Consensus	PoS, PoW, custom algorithms	Tendermint (BFT PoS)
Modularity	Fully modular (FRAME Pallets)	Modular but less customizable
Governance	On-chain governance & upgrades	On-chain voting
Upgradability	Forkless upgrades	Requires hard forks for major updates
Interoperability	Polkadot Parachains or Standalone	Cosmos IBC (Inter-Blockchain Communication)
Use Case	Highly customizable networks	Sovereign blockchains that need interoperability

When to Choose Substrate

If you need **a highly customizable blockchain** with control over consensus and governance.

If you prefer Rust's **performance and security guarantees**.

If you want **on-chain upgrades without hard forks**.

If you need **Polkadot compatibility**.

When to Choose Cosmos SDK

If you need **fast, sovereign blockchains** with **built-in staking and governance**.

If your project **requires interoperability with other blockchains via IBC**.

If you prefer a **simpler development experience with Go**.

If you need **quick finality and high transaction throughput**.

Both **Substrate and Cosmos SDK** are powerful tools for building **custom blockchains**.

Substrate is more flexible but requires deeper technical expertise in Rust.

Cosmos SDK is simpler to use and is ideal for blockchains that need **interoperability**.

The choice between **Substrate and Cosmos SDK** depends on your project's **goals, technical requirements, and need for customization**. Whether you need a **highly adaptable blockchain (Substrate)** or an **interoperable sovereign chain (Cosmos SDK)**, both frameworks provide the tools needed to build the next generation of decentralized networks.

Creating a Blockchain Node with Rust

A blockchain node is a fundamental component of a decentralized network. It is responsible for **storing the blockchain ledger, validating transactions, broadcasting new blocks, and communicating with other nodes**. A properly implemented blockchain node ensures **security, reliability, and scalability** in a distributed system.

Rust is an excellent choice for building blockchain nodes due to its **performance, memory safety, and concurrency model**.

A blockchain node operates as part of a **peer-to-peer (P2P) network**, where each node maintains a copy of the blockchain and follows **consensus rules** to validate new transactions and blocks.

Core Responsibilities of a Blockchain Node

Storing Blockchain Data: Keeps a record of all blocks and transactions in a structured database.

Networking: Connects with other nodes to exchange information.

Transaction Handling: Processes new transactions and verifies their validity.

Block Validation: Ensures that new blocks follow the consensus rules.

Consensus Participation: Engages in Proof of Work (PoW), Proof of Stake (PoS), or other mechanisms to agree on the chain state.

A node does not necessarily have to **mine blocks**; it can also act as a **full node**, which simply verifies transactions and propagates blocks across the network.

Setting Up the Rust Project

To begin, create a new Rust project:

```
cargo new rust_blockchain_node
cd rust_blockchain_node
```

Modify `Cargo.toml` to include the necessary dependencies:

```
[dependencies]
tokio = { version = "1", features = ["full"] }  #
Async networking
rocksdb = "0.19"  # Persistent storage
serde = { version = "1.0", features = ["derive"] }
# JSON serialization
serde_json = "1.0"
sha2 = "0.10"  # Cryptographic hashing
hex = "0.4"
```

These libraries will help with **networking, data persistence, serialization, and cryptographic hashing**.

Defining the Blockchain Structure

Each block contains essential information such as the **index, timestamp, transaction data, previous hash, and cryptographic proof**.

Modify `src/main.rs` to define the **Block structure**:

```
use sha2::{Sha256, Digest};
use serde::{Serialize, Deserialize};
use std::time::{SystemTime, UNIX_EPOCH};

#[derive(Serialize, Deserialize, Debug, Clone)]
```

```rust
struct Block {
    index: u64,
    timestamp: u128,
    data: String,
    previous_hash: String,
    nonce: u64,
    hash: String,
}

impl Block {
    fn new(index: u64, data: String, previous_hash:
String) -> Self {
        let timestamp = SystemTime::now()
            .duration_since(UNIX_EPOCH)
            .unwrap()
            .as_millis();

        let mut nonce = 0;
        let mut hash = String::new();

        while !hash.starts_with("0000") {  //
Adjust difficulty by changing zeros
            nonce += 1;
            let input = format!("{}{}{}{}{}",
index, timestamp, data, previous_hash, nonce);
            hash = format!("{:x}",
Sha256::digest(input.as_bytes()));
        }

        Block {
            index,
            timestamp,
            data,
            previous_hash,
            nonce,
            hash,
        }
    }
}
```

How This Works:

Each block is identified by its **index** and **timestamp**.

Transactions are stored as **data** in the block.

The **previous block's hash** ensures integrity.

Proof of Work (PoW) is implemented by requiring a hash that starts with `"0000"`, making mining computationally expensive.

Implementing the Blockchain Storage System

We need a **database system** to store blockchain data persistently. **RocksDB** is a fast key-value store that allows us to store and retrieve blocks efficiently.

Adding Blockchain Storage with RocksDB

Modify `src/main.rs` to include the blockchain structure:

```
use rocksdb::{DB, Options};

struct Blockchain {
    db: DB,
}

impl Blockchain {
    fn new(path: &str) -> Self {
        let db =
DB::open_default(path).expect("Failed to open
database");
        Blockchain { db }
    }

    fn add_block(&mut self, data: String) {
        let last_index =
self.db.iterator(rocksdb::IteratorMode::End).count(
) as u64;
        let previous_hash = if last_index == 0 {
            "0".to_string()
        } else {
            let last_block: Block =
serde_json::from_slice(

&self.db.get(last_index.to_string()).unwrap().unwra
p(),
            ).unwrap();
```

215

```
                last_block.hash
        };

        let new_block = Block::new(last_index + 1,
data, previous_hash);
        self.db.put(
            new_block.index.to_string(),

serde_json::to_vec(&new_block).unwrap(),
        ).unwrap();
    }

    fn get_blocks(&self) {
        for (_, value) in
self.db.iterator(rocksdb::IteratorMode::Start) {
            let block: Block =
serde_json::from_slice(&value).unwrap();
            println!("{:?}", block);
        }
    }
}
```

How This Works:

The blockchain is stored persistently using RocksDB.

Blocks are stored as key-value pairs, with the **block index as the key**.

The blockchain can be restarted without losing data.

Implementing Peer-to-Peer Networking

A blockchain node must **communicate with other nodes** to exchange transactions and blocks. **Tokio** is used to handle **asynchronous networking**.

Adding a Simple Peer-to-Peer Server

Modify src/main.rs to include networking:

```
use tokio::net::{TcpListener, TcpStream};
use tokio::io::{AsyncReadExt, AsyncWriteExt};

async fn handle_connection(mut stream: TcpStream) {
    let mut buffer = [0; 1024];
```

```
    let n = stream.read(&mut
buffer).await.unwrap();

    if n > 0 {
        println!("Received message: {}",
String::from_utf8_lossy(&buffer[..n]));
    }

    let response = "Message received".as_bytes();
    stream.write_all(response).await.unwrap();
}

#[tokio::main]
async fn start_server() {
    let listener =
TcpListener::bind("127.0.0.1:8080").await.unwrap();
    println!("Node running on 127.0.0.1:8080");

    loop {
        let (stream, _) =
listener.accept().await.unwrap();
        tokio::spawn(handle_connection(stream));
    }
}
```

How This Works:

The node listens on **port 8080** for incoming connections.

When another node connects, it **receives a message** and sends back a response.

Tokio's async runtime handles multiple connections efficiently.

Running the Blockchain Node

Finally, modify `main()` to initialize the blockchain and start the server:

```
#[tokio::main]
async fn main() {
    let mut blockchain =
Blockchain::new("blockchain_db");
```

```
    blockchain.add_block("Transaction: Alice ->
Bob: 10 BTC".to_string());
    blockchain.add_block("Transaction: Bob ->
Charlie: 5 BTC".to_string());

    println!("Blockchain state:");
    blockchain.get_blocks();

    // Start the node server
    start_server().await;
}
```

Run the program:

cargo run

This will:

Initialize the blockchain and store blocks persistently.

Start a peer-to-peer networking server on `127.0.0.1:8080`.

With Rust, we have built a **basic blockchain node** that:

Stores blocks using RocksDB for persistence.

Implements Proof of Work for mining.

Runs a P2P server to communicate with other nodes.

This foundation can be extended to include **transaction validation, consensus mechanisms, and full peer-to-peer block synchronization**, forming the basis of a **decentralized blockchain network**.

Implementing Governance and On-Chain Upgrades

Governance is an essential component of blockchain networks, allowing participants to **propose, vote on, and implement changes** without disrupting the system. Unlike traditional software, where updates are controlled by a central authority, blockchain governance ensures that **protocol changes, parameter adjustments, and feature upgrades** are managed in a

218

decentralized and transparent manner. Rust provides a powerful foundation for **building governance systems and handling on-chain upgrades** efficiently.

Governance in blockchain networks refers to the mechanisms that allow participants to **vote on changes, propose new features, and enforce rules** without requiring a central authority. Effective governance ensures that a blockchain **remains adaptable** to new challenges while maintaining security and decentralization.

Why Blockchain Governance is Important

Decentralization: Prevents control by a single entity and ensures **community-driven decision-making**.

Upgradeability: Enables the blockchain to **introduce new features, fix bugs, and improve efficiency**.

Security and Stability: Prevents unauthorized changes while allowing legitimate upgrades to be accepted **through consensus**.

Types of Blockchain Governance

Governance models vary depending on how decisions are made:

On-Chain Governance: Voting and decision-making happen directly on the blockchain. Participants use tokens or staking power to vote on proposals. Example: Polkadot, Tezos.

Off-Chain Governance: Discussions and decisions happen outside the blockchain (e.g., community forums, GitHub), and changes are implemented through software updates. Example: Bitcoin, Ethereum (before Ethereum 2.0).

Hybrid Governance: A combination of on-chain and off-chain decision-making. Example: MakerDAO, Cardano.

In this section, we will focus on **on-chain governance**, where votes and proposals are recorded directly in a **Rust-based blockchain**.

Implementing a Governance System in Rust

A **basic governance system** allows participants to:

Create proposals (e.g., change network fees, add new features).

Vote on proposals using tokens or staking power.

Execute approved proposals after meeting quorum requirements.

We will build a **simple governance system** that enables:

Submitting a proposal.

Voting on proposals.

Checking the status of proposals.

Executing approved proposals.

Step 1: Defining a Proposal Structure

Modify `src/main.rs` to define the governance system:

```
use std::collections::HashMap;
use serde::{Serialize, Deserialize};

#[derive(Serialize, Deserialize, Debug, Clone)]
struct Proposal {
    id: u64,
    description: String,
    yes_votes: u64,
    no_votes: u64,
    executed: bool,
}

impl Proposal {
    fn new(id: u64, description: String) -> Self {
        Proposal {
            id,
            description,
            yes_votes: 0,
            no_votes: 0,
            executed: false,
        }
    }

    fn vote(&mut self, support: bool) {
        if support {
```

```
                self.yes_votes += 1;
            } else {
                self.no_votes += 1;
            }
        }

    fn is_approved(&self) -> bool {
        self.yes_votes > self.no_votes  // Simple
majority rule
    }
}
```

Step 2: Implementing a Proposal Management System

Now, create a **governance manager** that handles proposals and voting:

```
struct Governance {
    proposals: HashMap<u64, Proposal>,
    proposal_count: u64,
}

impl Governance {
    fn new() -> Self {
        Governance {
            proposals: HashMap::new(),
            proposal_count: 0,
        }
    }

    fn create_proposal(&mut self, description:
String) -> u64 {
        let proposal_id = self.proposal_count;
        let proposal = Proposal::new(proposal_id,
description);
        self.proposals.insert(proposal_id,
proposal);
        self.proposal_count += 1;
        proposal_id
    }

    fn vote_on_proposal(&mut self, proposal_id:
u64, support: bool) -> Result<(), String> {
        match self.proposals.get_mut(&proposal_id)
{
```

```rust
            Some(proposal) => {
                proposal.vote(support);
                Ok(())
            },
            None => Err("Proposal not
found".to_string()),
        }
    }

    fn execute_proposal(&mut self, proposal_id:
u64) -> Result<(), String> {
        match self.proposals.get_mut(&proposal_id)
{
            Some(proposal) => {
                if proposal.is_approved() &&
!proposal.executed {
                    proposal.executed = true;
                    println!("Proposal {} executed:
{}", proposal_id, proposal.description);
                    Ok(())
                } else {
                    Err("Proposal not approved or
already executed".to_string())
                }
            },
            None => Err("Proposal not
found".to_string()),
        }
    }

    fn show_proposals(&self) {
        for proposal in self.proposals.values() {
            println!("{:?}", proposal);
        }
    }
}
```

Step 3: Running the Governance System

Modify main() to **test the governance module**:

```rust
fn main() {
    let mut governance = Governance::new();
```

```rust
    let proposal_id =
governance.create_proposal("Increase block
size".to_string());

    governance.vote_on_proposal(proposal_id,
true).unwrap();
    governance.vote_on_proposal(proposal_id,
true).unwrap();
    governance.vote_on_proposal(proposal_id,
false).unwrap();

    println!("Proposals before execution:");
    governance.show_proposals();


governance.execute_proposal(proposal_id).unwrap();

    println!("Proposals after execution:");
    governance.show_proposals();
}
```

Run the program:

cargo run

Expected output:

```
Proposals before execution:
Proposal { id: 0, description: "Increase block
size", yes_votes: 2, no_votes: 1, executed: false }

Proposal 0 executed: Increase block size

Proposals after execution:
Proposal { id: 0, description: "Increase block
size", yes_votes: 2, no_votes: 1, executed: true }
```

Enabling On-Chain Upgrades

On-chain upgrades allow a blockchain to **change its protocol without requiring a hard fork**. This is crucial for **long-term network maintenance and security improvements**.

How Rust Enables On-Chain Upgrades

Substrate Framework: Supports **forkless upgrades** via WebAssembly (Wasm).

Smart Contracts: Can be updated using governance mechanisms.

Upgradeable Modules: Rust-based blockchains can store **upgrade logic in runtime storage** and apply changes dynamically.

Example: Smart Contract Upgrade System

A blockchain can use a **governance vote** to deploy a **new contract version**:

```rust
struct UpgradeManager {
    version: u64,
}

impl UpgradeManager {
    fn new() -> Self {
        UpgradeManager { version: 1 }
    }

    fn upgrade(&mut self, new_version: u64) {
        if new_version > self.version {
            self.version = new_version;
            println!("Blockchain upgraded to
version {}", self.version);
        } else {
            println!("Invalid upgrade request");
        }
    }
}

fn main() {
    let mut upgrade_manager =
UpgradeManager::new();

    println!("Current version: {}",
upgrade_manager.version);
    upgrade_manager.upgrade(2);
    println!("Updated version: {}",
upgrade_manager.version);
```

Governance and on-chain upgrades ensure that blockchains remain **decentralized, adaptable, and secure**.

Governance mechanisms allow stakeholders to vote on changes without a central authority.

Rust-based blockchains can implement decentralized decision-making using simple voting systems.

On-chain upgrades prevent the need for disruptive hard forks, ensuring **seamless blockchain evolution**.

With these tools, developers can build **self-governing blockchains** that evolve efficiently while maintaining decentralization and security.

Chapter 12: Scaling and Optimizing Rust-Based Web3 Applications

Blockchain technology offers security, transparency, and decentralization, but these benefits come with challenges, especially in terms of **scalability and performance**. As networks grow, transaction speed, network congestion, and computational efficiency become critical concerns.

Rust is one of the most **efficient and high-performance programming languages**, making it an excellent choice for optimizing Web3 applications.

Layer 2 Scaling: Rollups, State Channels, Sidechains

Blockchain networks provide **security, decentralization, and immutability**, but they face a major limitation—**scalability**. As more users and applications interact with blockchains, networks become **congested, transactions slow down, and fees rise**. This is especially true for platforms like **Ethereum and Bitcoin**, where transaction throughput is limited due to **network consensus constraints**.

Layer 2 scaling solutions help **offload computation and storage from the main blockchain (Layer 1)** while maintaining the **security guarantees** of the base layer. These solutions include **rollups, state channels, and sidechains**, each providing different trade-offs between **scalability, security, and decentralization**.

Why Layer 2 Scaling is Necessary

Public blockchains like **Ethereum** can handle **only 15–30 transactions per second (TPS)**, while **Bitcoin** is limited to **7 TPS**. In contrast, traditional financial networks like **Visa** process **65,000 TPS**. The bottleneck occurs because every transaction must be **validated and recorded by all nodes** in the network.

A blockchain's security comes from its **consensus mechanism**, which requires **network-wide agreement on every transaction**. This ensures trust but severely limits throughput.

Layer 2 solutions **move computation off-chain** while ensuring that the **final transaction state remains secured by the base blockchain**. This dramatically improves performance while keeping the system decentralized and trustless.

Rollups: Scaling by Batching Transactions

Rollups improve blockchain scalability by **bundling multiple transactions** into a **single compressed transaction**, which is then submitted to the main blockchain. This significantly reduces the amount of **on-chain data** while maintaining **security and verifiability**.

How Rollups Work

Users send transactions to a **rollup operator**.

The operator processes these transactions **off-chain** and generates a **single proof of validity**.

The proof and the compressed transactions are **submitted to the main blockchain** for final settlement.

By reducing the number of transactions that need to be **fully verified and stored on-chain**, rollups increase throughput while maintaining **decentralization and security**.

Types of Rollups

Optimistic Rollups

Optimistic Rollups **assume transactions are valid by default** and only run verification **if fraud is suspected**. If someone challenges a transaction, the rollup performs **a fraud proof**, checking if the transaction was malicious.

Example of an Optimistic Rollup in Rust

```
struct Transaction {
    sender: String,
    receiver: String,
```

```rust
    amount: u64,
}

struct OptimisticRollup {
    transactions: Vec<Transaction>,
}

impl OptimisticRollup {
    fn new() -> Self {
        OptimisticRollup { transactions: Vec::new()
}
    }

    fn add_transaction(&mut self, tx: Transaction)
{
        self.transactions.push(tx);
    }

    fn submit_to_layer1(&self) -> String {
        let batch: Vec<String> =
self.transactions.iter()
            .map(|tx| format!("{}->{}:${}",
tx.sender, tx.receiver, tx.amount))
            .collect();
        format!("Batch Submitted: {:?}", batch)
    }
}

fn main() {
    let mut rollup = OptimisticRollup::new();
    rollup.add_transaction(Transaction { sender:
"Alice".to_string(), receiver: "Bob".to_string(),
amount: 10 });
    rollup.add_transaction(Transaction { sender:
"Charlie".to_string(), receiver:
"Dave".to_string(), amount: 20 });

    let result = rollup.submit_to_layer1();
    println!("{}", result);
}
```

Zero-Knowledge (ZK) Rollups

ZK-Rollups use **cryptographic proofs (ZK-SNARKs or ZK-STARKs)** to verify transactions **without revealing transaction details**. Every batch of transactions is submitted to the main blockchain along with a **validity proof**, ensuring security while preserving privacy.

Key advantages of ZK-Rollups:

No need for fraud challenges (unlike Optimistic Rollups).

Faster finality since transactions are verified instantly.

Example Use Case: **zkSync, StarkNet**

State Channels: Instant Transactions with Off-Chain Finality

State channels allow **participants to conduct multiple transactions off-chain**, only settling the final result on the main blockchain.

How State Channels Work

Two parties lock funds in a **multi-signature smart contract** on Layer 1.

Transactions occur **off-chain** and are signed by both parties.

Once the interaction is complete, the **final state is recorded on-chain**.

Since **every transaction does not need to be broadcasted**, state channels enable **near-instant and free transactions**.

Example: A Payment Channel Between Alice and Bob in Rust

```rust
struct StateChannel {
    balance_alice: u64,
    balance_bob: u64,
}

impl StateChannel {
    fn new(alice_initial: u64, bob_initial: u64) ->
Self {
        StateChannel { balance_alice:
alice_initial, balance_bob: bob_initial }
    }
```

```
    fn off_chain_transfer(&mut self, from_alice:
bool, amount: u64) {
        if from_alice {
            self.balance_alice -= amount;
            self.balance_bob += amount;
        } else {
            self.balance_bob -= amount;
            self.balance_alice += amount;
        }
    }

    fn settle_on_chain(&self) {
        println!("Settling on-chain: Alice: {},
Bob: {}", self.balance_alice, self.balance_bob);
    }
}

fn main() {
    let mut channel = StateChannel::new(100, 50);

    channel.off_chain_transfer(true, 10);
    channel.off_chain_transfer(false, 5);

    channel.settle_on_chain();
}
```

This system allows **instant transactions** between Alice and Bob until they decide to finalize the state **on the main blockchain**.

Real-World Use Cases

Bitcoin Lightning Network: Enables off-chain payments with near-zero fees.

Raiden Network (Ethereum): Facilitates instant token transfers.

Sidechains: Independent Chains for Scaling

Sidechains are **parallel blockchains** that connect to a main blockchain but operate independently. Unlike rollups and state channels, sidechains have their **own consensus mechanisms**, allowing them to scale while interacting with the main chain periodically.

How Sidechains Work

Users deposit assets into a **bridge smart contract** on the main blockchain.

These assets are **locked**, and an equivalent amount is minted on the sidechain.

Transactions occur on the sidechain, benefiting from **higher speed and lower fees**.

When users want to withdraw, they **burn the sidechain tokens** and reclaim assets from the main chain.

Example: Building a Simple Sidechain Connector in Rust

```rust
struct SidechainBridge {
    main_chain_balance: u64,
    sidechain_balance: u64,
}

impl SidechainBridge {
    fn new() -> Self {
        SidechainBridge { main_chain_balance: 1000,
sidechain_balance: 0 }
    }

    fn deposit_to_sidechain(&mut self, amount: u64)
{
        self.main_chain_balance -= amount;
        self.sidechain_balance += amount;
    }

    fn withdraw_to_mainchain(&mut self, amount:
u64) {
        self.sidechain_balance -= amount;
        self.main_chain_balance += amount;
    }
}

fn main() {
    let mut bridge = SidechainBridge::new();

    bridge.deposit_to_sidechain(100);
    println!("Sidechain Balance: {}",
bridge.sidechain_balance);
```

```
    bridge.withdraw_to_mainchain(50);
    println!("Mainchain Balance: {}",
bridge.main_chain_balance);
}
```

Examples of Sidechains

Polygon (Ethereum): Reduces congestion by processing transactions on a separate chain.

Rootstock (RSK) (Bitcoin): Enables smart contracts for Bitcoin.

Layer 2 solutions provide essential scalability improvements while **preserving decentralization and security**.

Rollups increase throughput by batching transactions.

State channels allow **off-chain transactions** for instant finality.

Sidechains run parallel to the main chain, optimizing speed and cost.

By integrating these solutions, developers can build **high-performance Web3 applications** without compromising blockchain security.

Performance Optimization in Rust for Blockchain

Blockchain networks require **high-speed transaction processing, efficient memory usage, and secure execution** to handle growing adoption and prevent bottlenecks. The decentralized nature of blockchain adds complexity, as **every transaction must be validated and stored permanently**. This makes performance optimization a **critical factor** in blockchain development.

Rust is a **high-performance systems programming language** that provides **zero-cost abstractions, memory safety, and concurrency control**, making it an ideal choice for **building scalable and efficient blockchain applications**.

Memory Safety and Optimization in Rust

Blockchain nodes store a large amount of **transaction history, smart contract state, and cryptographic proofs**. Memory efficiency directly impacts the **speed and scalability** of a blockchain system.

Rust eliminates **common memory issues** like **buffer overflows, null pointer dereferences, and use-after-free errors**, making it more secure than languages like **C++ or Go**.

Using Rust's Ownership Model for Efficient Memory Management

Rust's **ownership and borrowing system** ensures that blockchain data structures do not cause **unnecessary memory allocations** or **data races**.

Example: Efficiently managing blockchain state without cloning unnecessary data

```
struct Transaction {
    sender: String,
    receiver: String,
    amount: u64,
}

fn process_transaction(tx: &Transaction) {
    println!("Processing transaction from {} to {}
for {} coins", tx.sender, tx.receiver, tx.amount);
}

fn main() {
    let tx = Transaction {
        sender: "Alice".to_string(),
        receiver: "Bob".to_string(),
        amount: 100,
    };

    process_transaction(&tx); // Using a reference
avoids unnecessary cloning
}
```

This ensures that large transaction data structures are **passed efficiently** without redundant copies, reducing memory overhead.

Using Arc for Shared Data in Blockchain Nodes

Blockchain nodes frequently **share transaction data across multiple threads** for verification and consensus. Instead of **copying data**, Rust's **Arc (Atomic Reference Counting)** enables **safe and efficient shared ownership**.

Example: Using `Arc` for concurrent transaction processing

```rust
use std::sync::Arc;
use std::thread;

struct Transaction {
    sender: String,
    receiver: String,
    amount: u64,
}

fn main() {
    let tx = Arc::new(Transaction {
        sender: "Alice".to_string(),
        receiver: "Bob".to_string(),
        amount: 100,
    });

    let tx_clone = Arc::clone(&tx);
    let handle = thread::spawn(move || {
        println!("Processing transaction from {} to {} for {} coins", tx_clone.sender,
tx_clone.receiver, tx_clone.amount);
    });

    handle.join().unwrap();
}
```

By using **Arc**, we avoid **expensive cloning** while ensuring **thread safety**, which is crucial for multi-threaded blockchain nodes.

Optimizing Blockchain Networking with Rust's Asynchronous Runtime

Blockchain nodes communicate over a **peer-to-peer (P2P) network**, requiring **fast message propagation, low-latency transaction relaying, and parallel processing**. Rust's **Tokio runtime** provides **asynchronous networking**, ensuring high efficiency without blocking execution.

Using Asynchronous Networking for Transaction Broadcasting

Example: Implementing an async P2P transaction relay using Tokio

```
use tokio::net::{TcpListener, TcpStream};
use tokio::io::{AsyncReadExt, AsyncWriteExt};

async fn handle_connection(mut stream: TcpStream) {
    let mut buffer = [0; 1024];
    let n = stream.read(&mut
buffer).await.unwrap();

    if n > 0 {
        println!("Received transaction: {}",
String::from_utf8_lossy(&buffer[..n]));
    }

    let response = "Transaction
received".as_bytes();
    stream.write_all(response).await.unwrap();
}

#[tokio::main]
async fn main() {
    let listener =
TcpListener::bind("127.0.0.1:8080").await.unwrap();
    println!("Blockchain node listening on
127.0.0.1:8080");

    loop {
        let (stream, _) =
listener.accept().await.unwrap();
        tokio::spawn(handle_connection(stream));
    }
}
```

This allows multiple nodes to **send and receive transactions concurrently**, reducing **network congestion** while maintaining **high throughput**.

Implementing Efficient Blockchain Data Synchronization

When a new node joins the network, it must **synchronize blockchain history**. This process should be **optimized to prevent bottlenecks**.

235

Example: Rust-based blockchain state synchronization using async I/O

```
use tokio::fs::File;
use tokio::io::{self, AsyncReadExt};

async fn load_blockchain_state(file_path: &str) ->
io::Result<String> {
    let mut file = File::open(file_path).await?;
    let mut contents = String::new();
    file.read_to_string(&mut contents).await?;
    Ok(contents)
}

#[tokio::main]
async fn main() {
    let blockchain_data =
load_blockchain_state("blockchain_state.json").awai
t.unwrap();
    println!("Loaded blockchain state: {}",
blockchain_data);
}
```

Using **asynchronous file I/O**, blockchain nodes can **load state efficiently** without blocking execution.

Optimizing Blockchain Data Storage and Retrieval

Blockchain applications handle **large amounts of data**, including **transactions, account states, and smart contracts**. Efficient data storage ensures that **queries and updates remain fast**, even as the blockchain grows.

Using RocksDB for High-Performance Key-Value Storage

Rust's **RocksDB** integration allows blockchain nodes to **store and retrieve data efficiently**, ensuring fast block validation and transaction lookups.

Example: Storing blockchain transactions in RocksDB

```
use rocksdb::{DB, Options};

struct BlockchainStorage {
    db: DB,
}
```

```
impl BlockchainStorage {
    fn new(path: &str) -> Self {
        let db =
DB::open_default(path).expect("Failed to open
database");
        BlockchainStorage { db }
    }

    fn store_transaction(&self, tx_id: &str, data:
&str) {
        self.db.put(tx_id, data).unwrap();
    }

    fn get_transaction(&self, tx_id: &str) ->
Option<String> {
        match self.db.get(tx_id).unwrap() {
            Some(value) =>
Some(String::from_utf8(value).unwrap()),
            None => None,
        }
    }
}

fn main() {
    let storage =
BlockchainStorage::new("blockchain_db");

    storage.store_transaction("tx123", "Alice ->
Bob: 10 BTC");
    let tx_data =
storage.get_transaction("tx123").unwrap();
    println!("Retrieved transaction: {}", tx_data);
}
```

Using **RocksDB**, blockchain nodes can handle **millions of transactions** efficiently while maintaining **fast lookups**.

Parallel Transaction Processing for Scalability

Blockchain nodes must process **multiple transactions simultaneously** to achieve **high throughput**. Rust's **multi-threading model** ensures transactions are **validated and executed in parallel** without data races.

237

Using Rust's Rayon for Parallel Transaction Execution

Rayon provides **parallel iterators** that automatically distribute workloads across multiple CPU cores.

Example: Parallel transaction validation

```rust
use rayon::prelude::*;

struct Transaction {
    sender: String,
    receiver: String,
    amount: u64,
}

fn validate_transaction(tx: &Transaction) -> bool {
    tx.amount > 0
}

fn main() {
    let transactions = vec![
        Transaction { sender: "Alice".to_string(),
receiver: "Bob".to_string(), amount: 10 },
        Transaction { sender:
"Charlie".to_string(), receiver:
"Dave".to_string(), amount: 20 },
    ];

    let valid_transactions: Vec<_> =
transactions.par_iter()
        .filter(|tx| validate_transaction(tx))
        .collect();

    println!("Valid transactions: {}",
valid_transactions.len());
}
```

This ensures **multiple transactions are validated concurrently**, improving **throughput and scalability**.

Rust provides **exceptional performance and safety** for blockchain development.

Memory-efficient ownership and Arc-based data sharing prevent unnecessary cloning.

Async networking and I/O operations optimize transaction propagation and state synchronization.

High-speed key-value storage (RocksDB) enables efficient data retrieval.

Parallel processing with Rayon improves transaction throughput.

By leveraging these techniques, Rust-based blockchain applications achieve **faster execution, lower latency, and higher scalability**, making them **well-equipped for mass adoption**.

The Future of Rust in Web3

Web3 represents the **next evolution of the internet**, shifting away from centralized platforms and towards **decentralized, trustless, and user-controlled systems**. This transformation relies on **blockchain, cryptographic security, and decentralized applications (DApps)**. As Web3 technologies continue to grow, developers need programming languages that provide **security, performance, and reliability**.

Rust has emerged as one of the **most important languages for Web3 development**, offering a combination of **speed, memory safety, and concurrency control** that makes it well-suited for building **scalable and secure blockchain applications**.

Rust provides several advantages that make it well-suited for Web3 applications:

Memory Safety Without Garbage Collection

Traditional programming languages like **C and C++** allow for **manual memory management**, which can lead to **buffer overflows, segmentation faults, and security vulnerabilities**. In contrast, Rust uses **ownership and borrowing rules** to ensure **memory safety at compile time**.

Since **blockchain nodes run continuously**, avoiding memory leaks and runtime errors is critical. Rust's ability to **prevent crashes and ensure** stability makes it an ideal choice for building **long-running decentralized applications**.

High Performance for Blockchain Networks

Rust compiles directly to **machine code**, making it as fast as **C and C++** while avoiding **runtime inefficiencies**. Blockchains need **fast execution** to handle thousands of transactions per second (TPS), and Rust's low-level control over **memory and CPU usage** ensures optimal performance.

Unlike **JavaScript and Python**, which rely on **garbage collection**, Rust provides **predictable performance**, ensuring blockchain nodes do not experience **sudden execution pauses** that could impact transaction finality.

Concurrency for High-Throughput Applications

Blockchain networks require **multiple transactions to be processed in parallel** while maintaining security and correctness. Rust's **async programming model** (using **Tokio and async-std**) allows developers to build **highly concurrent applications** that can handle **thousands of network requests** efficiently.

For example, **Solana**, a high-speed blockchain capable of processing **over 50,000 TPS**, uses Rust to implement its **Proof of History (PoH) consensus algorithm**, which timestamps transactions before reaching consensus.

Security for Smart Contracts and Cryptography

Smart contracts are **self-executing agreements** that run on blockchains. These contracts must be **error-free**, as any vulnerability can be exploited permanently once deployed. Rust's **strict compiler checks and memory safety** make it an excellent choice for **developing secure smart contracts**.

Projects like **Ink! (for Polkadot) and Solana's Rust-based smart contracts** leverage Rust's **static type system** to prevent bugs at compile time, reducing the risk of costly exploits.

How Rust is Powering the Future of Web3

Rust's influence in Web3 development is growing rapidly, with several major blockchain ecosystems **adopting Rust as a primary language** for their infrastructure.

Rust in Blockchain Protocols

Many next-generation blockchain networks are **built entirely in Rust** due to its performance and security benefits:

Polkadot & Substrate: Polkadot, a multi-chain network designed for interoperability, is built using **Substrate**, a Rust-based blockchain framework that allows developers to create **custom blockchain networks** efficiently.

Solana: Known for its high throughput and low transaction costs, Solana relies on Rust to power its smart contract execution and validator nodes.

Near Protocol: A blockchain designed for developer-friendly DApps, Near uses Rust for its **runtime and smart contract execution**.

By choosing Rust, these networks ensure that **their blockchain engines are fast, secure, and scalable**.

Rust for WebAssembly (Wasm) Smart Contracts

WebAssembly (Wasm) is an emerging **lightweight binary format** that allows smart contracts to run **securely and efficiently** on blockchains. Rust is one of the best languages for compiling to **Wasm**, making it a leading choice for building **next-generation smart contracts**.

Examples of Rust-based Wasm contracts:

Ink! (Polkadot): A smart contract framework designed for Polkadot that compiles Rust code into Wasm.

CosmWasm (Cosmos): Enables cross-chain smart contracts for the Cosmos blockchain ecosystem.

Ethereum's Wasm (Ewasm): A future upgrade for Ethereum to improve smart contract execution using Wasm and Rust.

Rust's compatibility with **WebAssembly** means that developers can write **lightweight and highly efficient smart contracts** that are **portable across different blockchain networks**.

Rust in Zero-Knowledge Proofs and Cryptography

Zero-Knowledge Proofs (ZKPs) are **privacy-enhancing cryptographic techniques** that allow one party to prove knowledge of information **without revealing the information itself**. Rust is widely used for implementing **ZKP frameworks** due to its **performance and memory safety**.

Examples of Rust-based ZKP frameworks:

ZK-SNARKs (Halo2, Arkworks): Used in **Zcash** for private transactions.

ZK-Rollups (StarkNet, zkSync): Scalability solutions that bundle thousands of transactions into a **single proof**, dramatically reducing gas fees.

As privacy becomes a greater concern in Web3, Rust will play a **central role** in **secure cryptographic implementations**.

Decentralized Identity and Secure Data Storage

Web3 is shifting towards **user-controlled identity and decentralized data storage**. Rust is being used to develop **privacy-preserving identity systems** and **efficient distributed storage networks**.

Examples:

Self-Sovereign Identity (SSI): Rust-based identity frameworks like **Dock.io and Spruce ID** enable users to control their digital identity without relying on centralized authorities.

Decentralized Storage (IPFS & Arweave): Rust is used in storage protocols that provide **permanent, censorship-resistant data hosting**.

Rust ensures that **identity and storage systems** remain **secure, efficient, and resistant to data breaches**.

Emerging Trends in Rust-Based Web3 Development

Cross-Chain Interoperability

Future blockchain networks will need to **communicate seamlessly** across ecosystems. Rust-based protocols like **Polkadot, Cosmos (IBC), and Chainlink CCIP** are developing **trustless cross-chain bridges**, ensuring secure asset transfers between different blockchains.

Decentralized AI and Compute Networks

Rust is playing a role in **decentralized artificial intelligence (AI) and distributed compute** networks. Projects like **Golem and Aleph Zero** use Rust to create **secure, high-performance computation layers** for Web3 applications.

On-Chain Governance and Autonomous DAOs

Governance mechanisms in Web3 will increasingly rely on **smart contracts, on-chain voting, and automated decision-making**. Rust's ability to execute **secure governance protocols** is paving the way for **Decentralized Autonomous Organizations (DAOs)** with built-in upgradeability and transparency.

Rust is shaping the future of Web3 by providing:

Security and memory safety for blockchain nodes and smart contracts.

High performance and concurrency for scalable transaction processing.

Efficient WebAssembly support for next-generation smart contracts.

Advanced cryptographic frameworks for privacy-preserving applications.

As blockchain technology continues to evolve, Rust will remain at the forefront of **secure, scalable, and decentralized application development**. Developers looking to build **the next wave of Web3 innovations** should strongly consider Rust as their language of choice.

Conclusion

The evolution of **Web3 and blockchain technology** represents a fundamental shift in how digital systems operate, moving from **centralized control to decentralized, trustless environments**. This transformation brings new opportunities for **financial systems, governance, identity management, and decentralized applications (DApps)**. However, it also introduces significant **technical challenges**, including **scalability, security, and performance optimization**.

Throughout this book, we have explored **how Rust serves as a foundational language** for building **secure, efficient, and scalable** blockchain applications. From understanding **Rust's ownership model and concurrency features** to implementing **smart contracts, decentralized storage, and consensus mechanisms**, we have covered **key concepts and practical techniques** that developers need to create **robust Web3 solutions**.

Key Takeaways

1. Rust is the Future of Secure Blockchain Development

Rust provides **memory safety, zero-cost abstractions, and performance comparable to C++**, making it an **ideal choice for blockchain development**. Unlike languages that rely on **garbage collection**, Rust ensures **predictable execution times**, reducing the risk of **runtime vulnerabilities and unexpected performance bottlenecks**.

As blockchain networks grow in complexity, Rust's strict **type system and concurrency model** allow developers to write **highly secure and efficient code**, minimizing the risk of **exploits, data races, and smart contract vulnerabilities**.

2. Scalability and Performance are Critical for Web3 Adoption

The biggest challenge facing blockchain networks today is **scalability**. We explored **Layer 2 solutions like rollups, state channels, and sidechains**, all of which improve **transaction throughput and efficiency**.

Rust's **async programming model, parallel execution, and optimized data storage techniques** ensure that blockchain nodes can handle **thousands of transactions per second (TPS) without compromising security**. Projects like **Solana, Polkadot, and Near Protocol** have already demonstrated **how Rust-based blockchain architectures can achieve high-speed execution** while maintaining decentralization.

3. Decentralized Applications Require a Secure Backend and Frontend

Web3 applications **go beyond blockchain networks**—they require a **secure backend (Rust-based blockchain nodes) and a decentralized frontend**. We covered how Rust integrates with **WebAssembly (Wasm)**, allowing developers to write **efficient smart contracts** that execute **seamlessly across different blockchains**.

Additionally, we explored **how Rust interacts with JavaScript/TypeScript** for **frontend integration**, ensuring that **Web3 DApps provide a seamless user experience** while remaining decentralized.

4. Governance and On-Chain Upgradability Ensure Long-Term Sustainability

Unlike traditional software, **blockchain networks must evolve without centralized control**. We examined **on-chain governance models** that allow **token holders to propose and vote on protocol changes**, ensuring that blockchains remain **community-driven and adaptable**.

Rust-based frameworks like **Substrate (for Polkadot) and Cosmos SDK (for Cosmos)** enable **forkless upgrades**, allowing blockchains to **implement protocol changes without disrupting the network**. This makes **Rust-powered blockchain ecosystems more sustainable** in the long run.

5. Privacy and Security are Becoming Essential in Web3

Privacy is a growing concern in blockchain technology. We explored **Zero-Knowledge Proofs (ZKPs)** and **Rust-based cryptographic frameworks** that enhance **privacy and security** while maintaining decentralization.

Projects like **zkSync, StarkNet, and Aleo** are leveraging Rust's **performance and cryptographic capabilities** to develop **privacy-preserving smart contracts and transaction protocols**, ensuring that Web3 applications remain **secure and censorship-resistant**.

Web3 is still in its **early stages**, and its full potential is yet to be realized. As decentralized applications continue to expand, **Rust will play a major role in shaping the next generation of blockchain-based solutions**.

New consensus mechanisms and cryptographic innovations will require Rust's **efficiency and security**.

Cross-chain interoperability will become a key focus, with Rust-based protocols like **Polkadot, Cosmos, and Chainlink** enabling seamless communication between blockchains.

Decentralized AI and computing networks will use Rust to **optimize distributed processing and secure data sharing**.

Self-sovereign identity systems and decentralized finance (DeFi) applications will continue to leverage Rust's security guarantees.

By mastering **Rust and its application in Web3**, developers can contribute to **building the decentralized internet of the future**.

This book has provided a **comprehensive guide** to developing **secure, scalable, and efficient blockchain applications** using Rust. Whether you are **building a new blockchain, optimizing a decentralized application, or exploring new cryptographic techniques**, Rust equips you with the **tools and performance needed to push Web3 forward**.

As the Web3 ecosystem evolves, the demand for **Rust developers** will continue to grow. By applying the knowledge gained in this book, you are well-positioned to **develop cutting-edge blockchain solutions, improve the security of decentralized systems, and drive the future of Web3 technology**.

The decentralized future is being built today—Rust is helping make it faster, safer, and more efficient.

www.ingramcontent.com/pod-product-compliance
Lightning Source LLC
Chambersburg PA
CBHW080552060326
40689CB00021B/4827